T0339535

Cambridge Elements ≡

Elements in Politics and Society in Southeast Asia
edited by
Edward Aspinall
Australian National University
Meredith L. Weiss
University at Albany, SUNY

CONTESTING SOCIAL WELFARE IN SOUTHEAST ASIA

Andrew Rosser
University of Melbourne

John Murphy
University of Melbourne

CAMBRIDGE
UNIVERSITY PRESS

CAMBRIDGE
UNIVERSITY PRESS

Shaftesbury Road, Cambridge CB2 8EA, United Kingdom

One Liberty Plaza, 20th Floor, New York, NY 10006, USA

477 Williamstown Road, Port Melbourne, VIC 3207, Australia

314–321, 3rd Floor, Plot 3, Splendor Forum, Jasola District Centre, New Delhi – 110025, India

103 Penang Road, #05–06/07, Visioncrest Commercial, Singapore 238467

Cambridge University Press is part of Cambridge University Press & Assessment, a department of the University of Cambridge.

We share the University's mission to contribute to society through the pursuit of education, learning and research at the highest international levels of excellence.

www.cambridge.org
Information on this title: www.cambridge.org/9781108814362

DOI: 10.1017/9781108886642

First published 2023

A catalogue record for this publication is available from the British Library.

ISBN 978-1-108-81436-2 Paperback
ISSN 2515-2998 (online)
ISSN 2515-298X (print)

Contesting Social Welfare in Southeast Asia

Elements in Politics and Society in Southeast Asia

DOI: 10.1017/9781108886642
First published online: June 2023

Andrew Rosser
University of Melbourne

John Murphy
University of Melbourne

Author for correspondence: Andrew Rosser, andrew.rosser@unimelb.edu.au

Abstract: This Element argues that Southeast Asia's failure to develop stronger social protection systems has been, at its root, a matter of politics and power. It has reflected the political dominance within the region of predatory and technocratic elements, and the relative weakness of progressive elements. From the mid-1980s, democratisation, the emergence of political entrepreneurs seeking to mobilise mass electoral support and the occurrence of severe economic and social crises generated pressure on governments within the region to strengthen their social protection systems. But while such developments shifted policy in a more progressive direction, they have been insufficient to produce far-reaching change. Rather, they have produced a layering effect. Innovations have built upon pre-existing policy and institutional arrangements without fundamentally altering these arrangements, ensuring that social protection systems continue to have strong conservative, productivist and predatory attributes.

Keywords: Southeast Asia, politics, social protection, political settlements, welfare regimes

ISBNs: 9781108814362 (PB), 9781108886642 (OC)
ISSNs: 2515-2998 (online), 2515-298X (print)

Contents

1 Introduction

Improving social protection, especially for the poor and vulnerable, is one of the most important challenges facing Southeast Asian countries. Yet while Southeast Asian governments have introduced some important reforms during the past two and a half decades, they have invested relatively little in social protection by regional and international standards. At the same time, to the extent that they have invested in social protection, they have privileged segments of society such as civil servants, military officials and formal sector employees over the poor and vulnerable, and investments in education and to a lesser extent health over social security (see Section 1.1 for a more detailed discussion) (Cook and Pincus 2014; Sumarto 2020; United Nations Economic and Social Commission for Asia and the Pacific [UNESCAP] 2018a). In some cases, the effectiveness of social protection schemes in combatting poverty and vulnerability has also been undermined by corruption, skewing benefits towards the non-poor and reducing the quality and effectiveness of public services (Kim and Yoo 2015; Rosser 2012). As we will see in detail below, these patterns have continued despite the desperate circumstances created by the Covid-19 pandemic.

Why have Southeast Asian countries failed to develop stronger social protection systems? In particular, why have they failed to move beyond systems that privilege military and bureaucratic officials and, to a lesser extent, private sector workers to develop systems that provide adequate protection to the poor and vulnerable? Why have they simultaneously adopted important reforms in recent decades? What have been the main drivers of and obstacles to change, and how are they likely to shape the future evolution of social protection in the region?

This Element seeks to answer these questions through an analysis of the political dynamics shaping social protection in Southeast Asia. We argue that the region's failure to develop stronger social protection systems has reflected the political dominance within the region of predatory and, to a lesser extent, technocratic elements, and the relative weakness of progressive elements. This structure of power – or political settlement – has served to reinforce conservative tendencies embedded in social welfare models developed in the immediate post-colonial period, when politically important groups such as military and bureaucratic officials were given priority. It has also served to imbue social protection systems with attributes such as productivism – that is, prioritisation of economic growth over social policy goals (Holliday 2000) – and predation – that is, rent-seeking behaviour that can undermine the pro-poor intentions of social protection initiatives (Rosser and van Diermen 2018).

From the mid-1980s, democratisation led to the emergence of political entrepreneurs seeking to mobilise mass electoral support and opened up new opportunities for progressive elements to participate in and influence policy-making. These changes marked the emergence of more inclusive political settlements, albeit ones in which predatory elements remained dominant. Combined with the effects of the Asian Economic Crisis (AEC) of 1997–8, this generated new pressure on governments within the region to strengthen their social protection systems. Many responses shifted policy in a more progressive direction – that is, one informed by notions of human rights, equity and social justice – though they have been insufficient to produce a far-reaching restructuring of social protection. Rather, we have seen a layering effect, whereby innovations have built upon pre-existing policy and institutional arrangements without fundamentally altering these arrangements. While this sort of layering is not unusual in public policy (Streeck and Thelen 2005), it highlights the extent to which Southeast Asian social protection systems continue to have strong conservative, productivist and predatory attributes. The pandemic from early 2020 saw governments introduce new measures to address its severe health and economic impacts. These have likely produced a deepening and broadening of social protection coverage within the region, but possibly only on a temporary basis. There is little evidence so far to suggest that the pandemic has triggered marked changes in political settlements, constraining the prospects for more substantial change.

In presenting this argument, we begin by reviewing the evolution of social protection systems in the region, focusing on Indonesia, the Philippines, Thailand and Malaysia. We then outline a framework for understanding the political dynamics of social protection policy and its implementation, and for identifying the actors and interests that have shaped events and the agendas they have pursued. Then follow sections on our four focus countries examining the nature of their political settlements, and detailing how these and associated processes of contestation have shaped policy and its implementation in specific case study areas. The final section summarises the argument and considers possible trajectories of change.[1] Before beginning this analysis, however, it is necessary to benchmark the current state of poverty and vulnerability in the region as well as the extent of past social protection investment, briefly define several key terms and explain why we have chosen the four countries above as our focus.

---

[1] A note on sources: we have at times relied on desk-top research of media reports and government policy announcements, especially in our analysis of COVID-related policies. Rather than clutter the text with huge numbers of references to media reports, we have provided citations only where we directly quote from a media source or cite a specific item of information. Key media consulted include *Jakarta Post, Manila Standard, Bangkok Post*, antaranews.com, cnbc.com, channelnesasia.com, nationthailand.com, csis.org, irrawaddy.com, thaibsworld.com, malaysiakini.com, aseanbriefing.com, reuters.com, unicef.org, cnnphilippines.com and philstar.com.

1.1 Benchmarking Indicators

While rapid economic growth over several decades has led to markedly lower levels of poverty in the region, it has not eradicated poverty (Table 1). At the same time, millions of people remain 'near poor', with incomes leaving them vulnerable to falling back into poverty in the event of an economic crisis, natural disaster, or other shocks (Table 2). Many Southeast Asians also lack access to basic goods and services such as education and healthcare, clean energy, clean water, sanitation, nutritious food and secure livelihoods (UNESCAP 2018b: 24–43). In some Southeast Asian countries, these problems have been accompanied by rising inequality, producing tensions that threaten to undermine political and social stability and economic growth (Asian Development Bank [ADB] 2012). There has thus been a compelling need for Southeast Asian governments to introduce social protection programmes that provide households and individuals with support to avoid deprivation and social exclusion.

Yet social protection investment in Southeast Asia has been both low and skewed in favour of particular groups. This is evident in the ADB's Social Protection Indicator (SPI), which measures spending in the three categories of social protection: social insurance schemes to save for future needs, social assistance such as cash transfers and social pensions, and labour market programmes. Spending as a percentage of GDP per capita for each intended beneficiary for 2015 in each of these three categories is shown in Table 3, with aggregate spending providing the SPI. Asian countries overall recorded an average SPI of 4.0 per cent, with higher scores in the subregions of Central and West Asia (5.6) and East Asia (6.4). For the nine Southeast Asian countries included in the ADB's analysis the average SPI was much lower, at 2.6 per cent. While Malaysia, Singapore and Vietnam were well above this Southeast Asian average, and the Philippines was on the average, all other countries were well below average, including Indonesia and Thailand. Disaggregating these SPI scores into the separate categories shows the clear priority that has been given to social insurance (which often benefits civil servants and the military) over social assistance (which often targets the poor and vulnerable), and that there is negligible spending on labour market programmes. For example, almost all of Malaysia's high-level spending was on social insurance, much of it pensions for its civil service, with much smaller amounts for social assistance and nothing for labour market programmes.

Usefully, the ADB's SPI data also distinguishes between expenditure directed to the poor and the non-poor. While 19.2 per cent of total social protection spending was directed to the poor in Southeast Asia on average in 2015, in Malaysia the figure was only 6.8 per cent (of a larger total) while in the

Table 1 Poverty in Southeast Asia between the 1990s and today by available years: percentage of population living below US$1.90 per day (2011 PPP) and below national poverty line (NPL)

	US$1.90			NPL		
	1990s	2000s	Most recent	1990s	2000s	Most recent
Cambodia	na	na	na	na	50.2 (2003)	17.7 (2012)
Lao PDR	31.1 (1992)	25.7 (2007)	10.0 (2018)	na	na	18.3 (2018)
Myanmar	na	na	1.4 (2017)	na	48.0 (2005)	24.8 (2017)
Vietnam	52.3 (1992)	19.0 (2006)	1.8 (2018)	na	20.7 (2010)	6.7 (2018)
Timor Leste	38.5 (2001)	37.4 (2007)	22.0 (2014)	36.3 (2001)	50.4 (2007)	41.8 (2014)
Singapore	na	na	na	na	na	na
Brunei	na	na	na	na	na	na
Indonesia	54.9 (1990)	24.0 (2006)	2.2 (2021)	na	18.0 (2006)	9.8 (2020)
Malaysia	1.8 (1995)	na	0.0 (2015)	na	7.6 (2015)	8.4 (2019)
Philippines	13.7 (2000)	10.7 (2009)	2.7 (2018)	na	26.3 (2009)	16.7 (2018)
Thailand	9.2 (1990)	1.0 (2006)	0.0 (2020)	na	22.0 (2006)	6.8 (2020)

Notes:

1. Until 2019, Malaysia's National Poverty Line was regarded as very low, obscuring its poverty. From 2019, with a new methodology, the benchmark of income for the NPL more than doubled; hence the apparent rise in poverty between 2015 and 2019.

2. No figures are available for Singapore and Brunei in this dataset.

Source: World Bank, World Development Indicators, accessed 12 August 2022.

Table 2 Percentage and number of people in near poverty, by most recent available year, living below US$3.20 and US $5.50 per day (2011 PPP)

	A % @ $3.20	B % @ $5.50	C total population (relevant year)	Pop. @ $3.20 (AxC)	Pop. @ $5.50 (BxC)	Relevant year
Cambodia	na	na	16,250,000	na	na	2018
Lao PDR	37.4	70.4	7,062,000	2,612,940	4,943,400	2018
Myanmar	15.0	54.3	53,383,000	8,007,450	28,986,969	2017
Vietnam	6.6	22.4	95,546,000	6,306,036	21,402,304	2018
Timor Leste	65.9	91.8	1,219,000	803,321	1,119,042	2016
Singapore	na	na	5,639,000	na	na	2018
Brunei	na	na	429,000	na	na	2018
Indonesia	22	53	276,362,000	60,799,640	146,471,860	2021
Malaysia	0.3	2.9	30,271,000	90,813	877,859	2015
Philippines	17.0	46.9	106,651,000	18,130,670	50,019,319	2018
Thailand	0.3	6.4	69,800,000	209,400	4,467,200	2020

Source: World Bank, World Development Indicators, accessed 12 August 2022. No data are available for Singapore and Brunei.

Philippines it was 13.6 per cent. Indonesia and Thailand, though they had low total spending, spent proportionately more of it on the poor at 33.3 and 30.7 per cent respectively (ADB 2019: 89). These figures tell a story both of the slow development of social protection systems, and differences in the priorities of policy.

A similar pattern of Southeast Asian under-investment in social protection can be seen in International Labour Organization (ILO) data on public health and social protection expenditure as a share of GDP. Northern, Southern and Western European countries spent on average 18.7 per cent of GDP on social protection plus another 7.5 per cent on public health (a total of 26.2 per cent) in 2020 (or latest year available). These are obviously more mature welfare systems, but more recent entrants such as China and South Korea had total spending of over 10 per cent of GDP. By comparison, spending in ten countries in Southeast Asia averaged only 3.7 per cent: Vietnam (7.0), Malaysia (6.1) and Thailand (5.9) spent above average on both social protection and public health, while the Philippines (4.0) and Singapore (3.2) were close to the average. They were then followed by significant under-investors: Indonesia (2.7), Brunei (2.5), Cambodia (2.2), Lao PDR (1.6) and Myanmar (1.5) (ILO 2021: 278, 283–4). While these figures identify differences within the region, the overall pattern is of lagging development in social policy, resulting in highly uneven social protection coverage across occupational and income groups. According to UNESCAP and the ILO (2021: 15), only 33 per cent of the population in Southeast Asia benefits from at least one area of social protection.

1.2 Key Terms

We define *social protection*, following the United Nations Development Programme (UNDP 2016: 15–6), as: 'a set of nationally owned policies and instruments that provide income support and facilitate access to goods and services by all households and individuals at least at minimally accepted levels, to protect them from deprivation and social exclusion, particularly during periods of insufficient income, incapacity or inability to work'.

Social protection measures include (1) *social insurance*, meaning contributory 'public and private schemes providing insurance which protects income from life-course and work-related contingencies'; (2) *social assistance*, meaning non-contributory 'public programs and policies addressing poverty and vulnerability' such as cash transfer schemes, scholarship schemes for poor children and social pensions; (3) *labour market programmes* that aim to facilitate training and employment; and (4) *other measures that seek to enhance access to basic services* such as policies of free basic education (FBE) and free health care (Barrientos 2013: 24; UNDP 2016: 15–6). In our analysis, we distinguish between these *types* of social protection, as well as the *sectors* to which social protection schemes or programmes relate, with a particular focus on education, health and income support (financial assistance provided to the elderly, disabled, unemployed and other, usually disadvantaged, groups). Finally, we use *depth* of social protection to refer to the relative size of benefits, and *breadth* to refer to the proportion of the population covered by social protection programmes.

1.3 Case Selection

Our analysis focuses on Indonesia, Thailand, Malaysia and the Philippines for two reasons. The first has to do with demographics. These countries account for roughly three-quarters of the population of Southeast Asia and an even larger proportion of those in the region either living in poverty or vulnerable to poverty (Table 2). They are thus more central to the challenge of improving social protection systems in Southeast Asia than countries with smaller populations such as Singapore, Brunei, Timor Leste, Cambodia and Lao PDR, especially those – such as Singapore and Brunei – that are relatively wealthy. The second reason is that these four countries share much in common politically, making it possible to draw out common themes across the cases. All four have pursued capitalist (rather than communist or socialist) models of development, undergone extensive industrialisation, had extended periods of authoritarian or semi-authoritarian rule, experienced periods of democratic reform and inherited or developed oligarchic power structures.

A desire to focus on countries with common political characteristics is the main reason we exclude Vietnam and Myanmar from the analysis, two other countries that have both large populations and large numbers of people living in, or vulnerable to, poverty. As former socialist states their starting points, trajectories and political dynamics are quite distinct from those of our focus countries, notwithstanding that they have both shifted to more market-based systems since the end of the Cold War, and Vietnam has developed substantial social protection systems. This is a further reason for excluding Cambodia, which has a similar history.

Singapore has received much more attention in the literature on Asian welfare systems than any other Southeast Asian country, so our decision to exclude it from the analysis here may seem unusual. Research on its social policy development has frequently grouped it with a putative 'East Asian' (or in some versions 'Confucian') model of welfare, alongside Taiwan, Hong Kong,

South Korea and China (Peng and Wong 2010). While of interest, given its non-comparability with our four case study countries in sheer size, and given our focus on major challenges of development and poverty, we have elected to leave Singapore to one side.

It is worth noting that despite similarities our four focus countries differ in important respects. Despite being distinctly authoritarian with limited political freedoms, Malaysia has not experienced dictatorship, either in the overtly military form of Indonesia and Thailand, or in the form of support by the military (and martial law) as in the Philippines. Similarly, experiences of democratisation have differed: Indonesia, Thailand and the Philippines have undergone significant regime change from authoritarian to more democratic rule, then followed by some regression in Indonesia and the Philippines, while Thailand has reverted to military rule. In Malaysia, rather than a change of regime, democratic reform after the AEC took the form of a flowering of civil society and more energised and competitive opposition politics, leading to the electoral defeat of the long-dominant ruling coalition in 2018 with short-lived and unstable coalition governments since.

Finally, while our focus cases are all middle-income countries, Malaysia is, and has long been, a more developed capitalist economy. Its economic development path reduced poverty well before our other case studies embarked on the same task. Furthermore, as we detail below, Malaysia's starting point was markedly different because it inherited a relatively well-developed social protection system at independence. These similarities and differences matter for our analysis of the politics of social protection to the extent that our argument focuses on how oligarchic power structures, democratic reform and starting points have shaped social protection policy outcomes in the region.

2 The Evolution of Social Protection in Southeast Asia

In this section, we examine how social protection systems have developed in our four focus countries. We argue they have evolved through a layering effect and remain underdeveloped. Early initiatives provided pensions and health care for privileged groups through social insurance and introduced FBE. These initiatives were then overlaid with more inclusive systems of social insurance, expanded access to free health care and programmes of social assistance targeting the poor and vulnerable. Despite these changes, however, significant gaps in the breadth and depth of social protection remain, while some initiatives have experienced serious problems in implementation, including non-compliance, and misallocation due to poor administration, absence of key data and corruption. Our discussion is organised according to types of social protection and focuses initially on the period up to the Covid-19 pandemic. It then examines government responses to the pandemic and their implications for social protection arrangements. The Appendix provides a timeline of the evolution of each country's social protection system.

2.1 Social Insurance

Early in the evolution of their social protection systems, all four of our focus countries introduced social insurance arrangements, in which employees and employers were mandated to contribute to saving for retirement, and other benefits such as sickness, disability and health insurance. Each country initially attended to the interests of state employees – civil servants and the armed forces. Thailand was the first, establishing a generous pension scheme in 1902 for civil servants, funded entirely by the state and requiring no contributions. Malaysia, by independence in 1957, had an equivalent pension also fully funded by the state. Strictly speaking, these pensions were not 'social insurance', as they did not require contributions by state employees. They promised generous defined benefit pensions, paid from general revenue. In 1996, the Thai government managed to trim this level of generosity by restructuring the system as it applied to new entrants, requiring a small contribution from their salaries, and limiting their entitlement to a defined contribution pension (Chuen 2019).[2]

The equivalent civil service pensions in the Philippines (from 1936) and Indonesia (from 1963), are more accurately described as 'social insurance', because they involve regular contributions by employees, in both cases with the state paying a defined benefit pension, along with other benefits. The Philippines Government Service Insurance System was based on 9 per cent of salary from employees, matched by 12 per cent from the government, part of which was for life insurance (World Bank 2018a). In Indonesia, the civil service pension collected employee contributions of only 8 per cent; the government did not make actual contributions, but simply guaranteed a defined benefit pension. The numbers benefitting from these pensions are small, ranging from about 3 per cent of the labour force in Thailand, to up to 11 per cent in Malaysia in recent years. But the costs are considerable, and represent a redistribution from general government revenue to the privileged. In 2018, Malaysia's civil service pensions consumed 10.8 per cent of the budget; in Indonesia, in 2013, the equivalent for civil service retirees was 4.5 per cent (Choong and Firouz 2020; Handra and Dita 2016).

---

[2] 'Defined benefit' systems provide a guarantee of the value of the pension, usually relative to salary, while 'defined contribution' systems only provide a pension based on the investment value of contributions made.

Parallel systems for the armed forces as state employees were separated out from these civil service schemes in 1939 in Thailand, 1971 in Indonesia and 1972 in Malaysia. Information about military pensions is sketchy, reflecting a reluctance on the part of state authorities to disclose details. It appears the Indonesian and Thai systems have the same arrangement as for civil servants with regard to contributions and benefits, but the Malaysian scheme requires contributions from armed forces personnel and pays only a defined contribution pension at the age of fifty. At the turn of the millennium, the Philippine military scheme was reportedly bankrupt with pensions being paid entirely from the Ministry of Defence's budget (Asher and Bali 2012; Pineda 2019).

Health benefits for civil servants, the military and their families have usually been included as part of these pension schemes, though in Indonesia civil servants' health insurance was established as a separate scheme in 1968.

There is a scarcity of research describing the politics leading to these first systems of social protection. Malaysia's early development of state pensions (and its Employees' Provident Fund and health systems discussed below), came out of its colonial past, particularly the period immediately before independence when Labour was in power in Britain. In Indonesia, the Philippines and Thailand, the early development of generous benefits for civil servants and the military reflected a common pattern in authoritarian regimes which needed to stabilise the support and loyalty of key groups; the same pattern has been noted in Korea and Taiwan (Peng and Wong 2010), and in post-colonial states in the Middle East and North Africa (Karshenas et al. 2014).

The model of social insurance was then widely used in the next stage of social protection systems for formal sector wage workers in private firms and state-owned enterprises. The recurring pattern was that states established compulsory social security schemes to which both employers and employees contributed, saving for pensions (or lump sum retirement payments) and providing other occupational benefits such as work injury insurance, and sometimes sickness benefits and health insurance. Malaysia's Employees' Provident Fund (EPF), established in 1949, was the earliest, while the Philippines' Social Security System followed in 1957, and was made mandatory in 1960. Thailand failed twice to establish a social security system (in 1939 and 1954) due to significant employer resistance; it was finally legislated in 1990. Indonesia was a laggard, developing its equivalent scheme, *Jamsostek*, in 1992.

In each case, enrolled workers' contributions from wages were matched by employers, though the rates of contribution varied. The Malaysian system started with low rates, but from the 1990s these were increased to 12 per cent (employer) and between 8 and 11 per cent (employees). In Thailand, the rates were 5 per cent for both, topped up by another 2.25 per cent by the state. In the Philippines, they were 7.4 per cent (employer) and 3.6 per cent (employee), though only 6 per cent went to retirement savings. Indonesia had the lowest rates of contribution at only 3.7 per cent (employer) and 2 per cent (employee) (Park 2012).

These social insurance schemes for private sector workers reflect what Holliday (2000) described as a 'productivist' strategy, providing social protection to a group seen as central to economic development. But there are general patterns of under-subscription through evasion, and inadequate savings for retirement. Non-compliance – by both workers and employers – stemmed from unwilling-ness to pay, lack of confidence in the adequacy of pension benefits and, particu-larly in Indonesia, concern the accumulated funds would be plundered by corrupt elites. As Wisnu (2007: 204–8) noted, *Jamsostek* 'served as a giant piggy bank', and in 2005 an executive director of the scheme was jailed for illegal investment. As a result, evasion was widespread and by 2012, after twenty years' operation, the Indonesian system covered merely a quarter of formal sector workers, or as little as 10 per cent of the labour force. By 2008, the Thai scheme covered only 23 per cent of the workforce, while the equivalent scheme in the Philippines covered some 33 per cent of the labour force in 2016. The Malaysian system was most successful in ensuring participation, covering some 43 per cent (Asher 2009; Handra and Dita 2016; World Bank 2018b).

Furthermore, relatively low levels of required contributions have meant retire-ment savings are inadequate for those who have participated. Even in the most successful of these schemes – Malaysia's EPF – savings are low, in part because thirty per cent of savings can be withdrawn early to fund housing, education and some health expenses; the remainder – especially for low-wage earners – has not been enough to fund retirement. World Bank studies have found that half of those Malaysians who had taken a lump sum at retirement had exhausted their savings in five years (2018b), and that the savings of almost three-quarters of current EPF participants would only pay a pension of half the national poverty line (2020a). Poverty among EPF retirees is especially reported if they had been low-wage and/ or female workers who made small contributions and had intermittent participa-tion (Vaghefi et al. 2017). Increased contribution rates from the 1990s, and reforms to gradually increase the retirement age, may lead to a better future in Malaysia, but it is salutary to think that even in the most advanced and modern-ised of our case studies, formal sector retirement savings are so inadequate. The pensions available through compulsory savings in Indonesia, the Philippines and Thailand are even less adequate, because the contribution rates are so low.

Social insurance has been the model widely used in European welfare states; in the advice from international agencies, it has often been assumed to be the only model. But the experience of our case study countries demonstrates two recurring problems: first, evasion and non-compliance cannot be sufficiently policed; and second, even where compliance is achieved, many workers cannot afford, and many employers resist, contribution rates high enough to produce adequate savings. A third and obvious problem is that the social insurance model can only work for the formal sector. Where the informal sector is large, as in Indonesia, the Philippines and Thailand, the social insurance model cannot reach the bulk of the working population who have no formal employment relationship, and no formal wage. The World Bank for some time spoke of numbered 'pillars' of retirement insurance, distinguishing between compulsory or not, and employment-based or private savings. It was only in 2005 that they recognised another option – a tax-funded, targeted social pension, as social assistance – which was then dubbed the 'zero pillar' (Holzman and Hinz 2005).

2.2 Social Assistance

As seen in Table 3, our four focus countries have in general invested much less in social assistance than social insurance. This lack of investment is particularly apparent with regard to protection against unemployment and assistance for disability. There are some small programmes in each area in our focus countries but they are very underdeveloped. In other areas of social assistance such as social pensions and cash transfers, governments are doing more but the extent and nature of their programmes vary considerably across the region.

Table 3 Social protection indicator by category, as % of GDP, 2015

	Social insurance	Social assistance	Labour market programmes	SPI overall
Cambodia	0.1	0.5	–	0.6
Lao PDR	0.7	0.1	–	0.8
Myanmar	0.1	–	–	0.1
Vietnam	3.6	0.4	0.1	4.1
Singapore	4.8	1.1	0.3	6.2
Indonesia	1.4	0.6	0.1	2.1
Malaysia	4.3	0.1	–	4.4
Philippines	1.8	0.8	–	2.6
Thailand	1.7	0.5	–	2.2
Southeast Asia average	2.0	0.5	0.1	2.6
Asia average	3.1	0.9	0.1	4.0

Source: ADB (2019: 84).

2.2.1 Social Pensions

All our case study countries have developed a social pension as a tax-funded transfer to the elderly poor, but with varying levels of breadth and to a lesser extent depth (Table 4). In Indonesia, the Social Assistance for Older Persons (ASLUT) scheme is of benefit to a miniscule proportion of the elderly, is focussed on the bedridden, and provides very modest benefits. Malaysia's *Bantuan Orang Tua* social pension also has very little breadth. Asher (2009: 274–5) has noted that Malaysia's retirement policy system has remained largely unchanged for half a century and has not made the transition to settings 'more commensurate with its high middle-income country status'. The social pension, first established in 1982, is only available to about 5 per cent of the aged, targeted to those over sixty with no fixed income and no family support. The payment of RM350 per month is low, about 16 per cent of a national poverty line, though that is more generous than in neighbouring countries.

Thailand and the Philippines both have more expansive social pensions in terms of breadth. When introduced in 1993, the Thai Old Age Allowance (Case Study 7.2) was targeted to the poor aged over sixty, but evidence of widespread misallocation through local patronage networks discredited the idea of targeting and led to it being made universal in 2009. By 2017, almost 72 per cent of the aged population was receiving the payment, with more recent reports of up to 85 per cent. But the monthly amount – which increases with age – is low, equivalent to between 7.6 and 12.6 per cent of the national poverty line (Suwanrada et al. 2018). The Philippines' Social Pension (Case Study 6.1) was introduced in 2010, and intended to be rigorously targeted to the poor. It is a very small monthly payment equivalent to about 4.7 per cent of national poverty line. At first, it was directed only to the 'indigent and infirm' aged eighty or over, but then extended in a series of steps; by 2016, it included those aged sixty or over. It has very significant misallocation, with many of the wealthy also receiving it, due to local patron–client networks distorting decisions on eligibility (Velarde and Albert 2018).

While social insurance cannot work for the informal labour force, the alternative model – social assistance targeting cash benefits to the poor – can work only when the targeting works, in terms of both accurately identifying the poor and excluding the non-poor. Thailand responded to the failure of targeting by making the payment universal, but that tends to keep the rate of payment low, because the cost of any increase would be considerable. The Philippines has stuck with a badly targeted pension, with spectacular exclusion and inclusion error. Despite these problems, at least Thailand and the Philippines have cash transfer systems that include the elderly poor. A realistic social pension is

Table 4 Social pensions in Southeast Asia

	Year introduced	Number of pensioners	'Breadth' as % of aged pop.	'Depth': est. value as % of US$1.90 poverty line	'Depth': est. value as % of national poverty line
Indonesia: *Asistensi Social Usia Lanjut* (social assistance for older persons)	2006	26,500	0.1	15.6	9.5
Malaysia: *Bantuan Orang Tua* (elderly assistance scheme)	1982	120,496 to 144,000	est. 4 to 5.5	87.2	15.9
Philippines: social pension scheme	2011	2,800,000	35.4	10.4	4.7
Thailand: old age allowance	1993	8,048,298	71.8	18.7 to 31.1	7.6 to 12.6

Notes:

1. Figures for number and per cent of beneficiaries from ILO 2017, Table B.10, reflecting circa 2015.

2. Poverty lines derived from World Bank databank and specific country reports, accessed 19 December 2021.

3. The Old Age Allowance increases with age in Thailand.

4. Indonesia added some payments for the elderly over seventy to its PKH family cash transfer programme in 2016.

5. Authors' estimates of (pre-Covid) pension values relative to poverty lines should be treated with caution. Dates for poverty lines and for reported values of the pension do not always align; and we have converted the austere US$1.90 per person per day poverty line to a poverty line for a household of four (also used in Table 5), which underestimates the value of the pension to a single elderly individual (if alone). Nevertheless, estimates allow for comparison of the relative value or depth of these social pensions.

missing in both Malaysia and Indonesia, leaving families to take on support for the elderly poor more or less on their own.

2.2.2 Cash Transfers

Each of our four focus countries has developed cash transfer programmes since the AEC. These fall into two main categories – conditional (CCT) and unconditional cash transfers (UCT). In the former, payments are conditional on the beneficiary's actions, while in the latter they are simply targeted cash grants. The main programmes are summarised in Table 5.

In the Philippines, the *Pantawid* programme (Case Study 6.1), first launched as a pilot in 2007, provides monthly payments increasing with the number of children, with conditions relating to school attendance and basic health checks. It is a large programme, delivered to some 4.5 million households, and the payments are relatively generous, ranging from 4.7 up to 28 per cent of the national poverty line, depending on family size. Despite criticisms of how it is allocated, and specifically about the incidence of corruption, the targeting has not been as spectacularly wayward as for the social pension (Dadap-Cantal et al. 2021; Sicat and Mariano 2021).

Indonesia developed UCTs from 2000, seeking to compensate the poor for increased fuel prices as fuel subsidies were reduced. While they were substantial, UCT programmes – in 2000, 2005, 2009 and 2013 – were explicitly temporary. In parallel, a CCT programme, the Family Hope Program (PKH), was developed from 2007. This now covers some ten million households with school-age children. It provides a base payment and added benefits for schooling; the amounts available are considerably less than in *Pantawid*. Payments for family members with a disability or for the elderly were added in 2016. In addition, an earlier system of selling subsidised rice to the poor (*RASKIN* and later *RASTRA*) was replaced from 2017 with a cashless card scheme (*Program Sembako*), funding purchases of staple foods including rice (Cahyadi et al. 2020; Kwon and Kim 2015). Indonesia's long-standing PKH programme is a significant budgetary commitment representing about 1.3 per cent of government spending, and is generally considered to be targeted effectively. After early failures and elite capture, Indonesia has developed the capacity to deal with the technical challenges of accurately identifying the poor, largely due to building expertise in institutions such as the National Team for the Acceleration of Poverty Reduction (TNP2 K) and the SMERU research institute, a think tank conducting applied social research (Bah et al. 2019; Hardjono et al. 2010).

Thailand has smaller and much more recent cash transfer programmes. From 2015, a Child Support Grant has delivered modest payments to poor families with

Table 5 Cash transfer programmes in Southeast Asia

	First introduced		'Breadth' est. number of beneficiaries	'Depth' est. value as % of US$1.90 poverty line	'Depth' est. value as % of national poverty line
Indonesia: *Program Keluarga Harapan* (family hope program)	2007	Conditional	10 mill. households	3.9 to 14.3	2.4 to 8.7
Program Sembako cashless card for staple food purchases	2017	Unconditional	15.2 mill. households	15.6	9.5
Malaysia: BR1M/*Bantuan Sara Hidup*	2012	Unconditional	7.1 mill. households	124.5 to 249.1	22.6 to 45.3
Philippines: *Pantawid Pamilyang Pilipino Program*	2007	Conditional	4.5 mill. households	10.4 to 62.4	4.7 to 28.0
Thailand: child support grant – children to age 3	2015	Unconditional	est. 1.4 mill. households	18.7	7.6
Welfare card – cashless card for designated purchases	2017	Unconditional	est. 11 mill.	6.2 to 9.3	2.5 to 3.8

Notes:

1. Ranges of payments reflect different family size, and in Malaysia also vary with income groups within the bottom 40 per cent of households.

2. Authors' approximate estimates of value of (pre-Covid) payments, relative to the austere World Bank poverty line (US$1.90 per capita per day) and official national poverty lines for households; see note to Table 4.

3. Estimates of (pre-Covid) numbers of beneficiaries are derived from multiple sources.

infants aged up to 3, and from 2017, a cashless welfare card has allocated small amounts for designated purchases at registered shops. Table 5 shows the amounts paid are relatively small. Finally, Malaysia developed an UCT programme in 2012 (since 2019 called *Bantuan Sara Hidup*) in the context of significant cuts to fuel subsidies (Case Study 8.2). It is targeted to the poorest 40 per cent of households ('B40' – bottom 40 per cent), based on household income. The maximum payments to the poorest families can be up to 45 per cent of the national poverty line, meaning that when it does reach the poorest of the population, BSH has real depth. In this respect, it is the most significant cash transfer programme among our case studies (Choong and Firouz 2020; World Bank 2020a).

In conclusion, while many of these social assistance programmes are very modest payments, and vary in their breadth, all of our focus countries have developed mechanisms for delivering resources to the poor. These were then available to be used during the pandemic response.

2.3 Labour Market Programmes

As Table 3 shows, spending on labour market programmes in our focus countries is generally too small to register in international organisations' statistics. The ADB's assessment that labour market programmes are 'the most underresourced area of social protection in Asia' is generally shared. But there is some ambiguity about what is included in this type of social protection. For the ADB, it includes 'help for people to secure employment', and 'skills development and training' which 'play a crucial role in improving the existing skills supply and promoting inclusion in the labour market' (2019: xii, 2 & 73). But the ADB also includes public works – such as cash for work initiatives – which the World Bank classifies as part of social assistance. Unemployment insurance benefits such as have recently been added in Malaysia are generally seen as part of social insurance. Indonesia has developed a 'Pre-Employment' programme, providing online skills training and a small payment for the unemployed, and also has some cash for work programmes under its Village Fund. The Philippines has small entrepreneurship support and training programmes targeted to informal sector workers such as pedicab operators, farmers and fishers, and has also used public works programmes to support displaced workers (World Bank 2018a). But in general, this area of social protection is widely noted as underdeveloped in the region.

2.4 Other Types of Social Protection

2.4.1 Free Basic Education

Each of our focus countries adopted policies providing for FBE early in the development of their social protection systems. Initially, they concentrated on free education at the primary level but, over time, sought to extend it to the secondary level.

In the Philippines, FBE policy has its origins in the colonial period. The American colonial authorities guaranteed free compulsory education under the 1898 Constitution and established a free public school system (Case Study 6.2). Subsequent Constitutions provided for free and compulsory education at least at the elementary level, and in the late 1980s, free education was extended to the secondary level.

In Malaysia, FBE policy also has its origins in the colonial period, when the British established free primary schools for rural ethnic Malays (Lee 1997). After independence, the government continued to privilege ethnic Malays, granting them free tuition at both Malay-medium and non-Malay-medium primary schools. In 1962, it ended this disparity by granting free tuition to non-Malay citizens in non-Malay-medium primary schools. During the remainder of the 1960s, it extended free education to the secondary and tertiary levels for Malay citizens (Rudner 1977). Over time, it extended free secondary education to non-Malays, creating an education system in which education is free for all citizens from kindergarten to upper secondary school (ASEAN 2013).

Indonesia formally introduced FBE in 1977, when it officially abolished fees at government primary schools. It extended this policy to government junior secondary schools in 1994. Following decentralisation in 2001, some regional governments used their new authority to make upper secondary education free (Case Study 5.1).

In Thailand, FBE has its origins in developments following the transition to constitutional monarchy in 1932. These included compulsory primary school-ing for four years, and commitments to develop education; compulsory school-ing was extended to six years in 1960 (Sirindhorn 2018). In 1978, a new constitution mandated that compulsory education should be universal and free. In 1997, another new constitution provided that all Thais are entitled to twelve years of free and quality education. In 2009, the Ministry of Education extended this period to fifteen years (ASEAN 2013).

Despite their long history of free education, and gradual extension from the primary to secondary levels, such policies have not necessarily led to FBE in practice. On the one hand, free education has generally only meant exemption from tuition fees rather than the wider costs associated with education (e.g. transport, textbooks, uniforms). On the other hand, fees have often persisted as underfunding and corruption have led to pressure on parents to pay non-tuition-related fees, illegal fees and 'voluntary' contributions to schools or parent teacher associations. Nevertheless, FBE policies appear to have lowered the cost of education in our four focus countries and contributed – along with rising income levels due to economic growth, and efforts by governments to build schools, recruit teachers and more generally expand public education – to a huge increase in school enrolment levels in recent decades.

2.4.2 Universal Health Coverage (UHC)

Our case study countries have converged – at very different paces – towards commitments to UHC, but with important differences in how their health systems have evolved.

Malaysia inherited a national health system from the colonial period, with free basic care in rural areas, and highly subsidised care for everyone else, as well as public hospital care. This was an exceptional position to be in at the beginning of the post-colonial period. Free health care has been a significant part of the political relationship between UMNO and the *Bumiputera* (indigenes), and popular support for the system has understandably been an obstacle to attempts to partly privatise it, or to introduce mandatory insurance; citizens have defended the public goods they have against attempts to diminish them (Case Study 8.1).

Elsewhere in the region, universal health care has been a late developer, though the prominence it is now given by international agencies has elevated it in policy discussions. Health policy has been a salient issue in post-authoritarian politics in Thailand, the Philippines and Indonesia; promising health care has been attractive under conditions of more democratic politics.

The Philippines system (PhilHealth) developed slowly from 1995, gradually expanding from the compulsory insurance system for waged workers. From 2011, President Benigno Aquino III extended free coverage to the aged and poor (Capuno et al. 2021). By mid-2021, coverage was almost universal, with some 39 per cent of the population being 'indirect contributors', whose free access is funded by the state. The fiction here is that it is still health 'insurance', but the poor have free access because their 'premiums' are paid by the state. Thailand took a different path to the same result, with UHC (with a small co-payment) expanded in one dramatic burst in 2001–2. Developed as a detailed policy by progressive health bureaucrats and civil society activists, it helped to win Thaksin Shinawatra the support of the rural poor in the 2001 election (Case Study 7.1).

By contrast, Indonesia's health insurance was much slower to develop. Health coverage for some of the poor was part of the Social Safety Net after the fall of Suharto, and in the mid-2000s health coverage for the uninsured was expanded by both central *Askeskin/Jamkesmas* and provincial *Jamkesda* schemes. These initiatives have been widely seen as part of a more democratic polity, with health a salient issue in the electoral appeal of both old and new elites. From 2014, the existing schemes were rolled into one as *Jaminan Kesehatan Nasional* (JKN), with the intention of universal coverage (Case Study 5.2).

This expansion towards UHC has been a significant development in Thailand, the Philippines and Indonesia in the last three decades, though political and budgetary challenges remain. Governments need to provide enough funding to cover the notional 'insurance premiums' of the poor, there are still some left uninsured in the 'missing middle' and access is only a part solution if the quality and distribution of health services remains poor.

2.5 A Note on Migrant Workers

Both Thailand and Malaysia have large cohorts of migrant workers, who are excluded from social protection. Estimates of the migrant workforce, a majority of whom are women, are between 10 and 13 per cent of the Thai workforce, and 14 to 16 per cent of Malaysia's workforce. Both countries have unknown, but substantial, numbers of undocumented migrant workers; a recent estimate for Malaysia was that there were 2.2 million registered migrant workers and another 3.3 million who were undocumented (ILO 2020). None are covered by existing pension savings, health insurance or cash transfer systems, though in Thailand they are required to take out private health insurance, and in Malaysia they have recently been better covered for workplace injury insurance (ILO-UN Women Collaboration 2015; Low 2021). Policymakers might claim that a migrant workforce can be excluded from social protection because such policy is only for citizens, but having a significant, cheap and exploited underclass at the bottom of the labour market is a way of ensuring that citizens of Malaysia and Thailand are not themselves at the bottom. In both countries, migrant workers were the first to suffer the economic impact of the pandemic.

2.6 Responses to Covid

Covid had devastating effects in Southeast Asia; according to the World Health Organisation (WHO), by September 2022 our four focus countries had suffered just under 20 million confirmed cases and 288 thousand deaths (WHO 2022). The pandemic was also a major economic crisis, reducing economic activity and trade, and threatening widespread unemployment and poverty. The ADB calculated that in 2020 the Philippines' economy contracted by 9.6 per cent, followed by Thailand (6.1 per cent), Malaysia (5.6 per cent) and Indonesia (2.1 per cent) (ADB 2021). All countries, including in Southeast Asia, implemented economic and monetary policies to keep their economies afloat, creating credit, buying equity and easing

Table 6 Estimates of new poverty in 2020 as a result of
the pandemic:
Percentage of population newly poor resulting from the
pandemic at poverty lines of US$1.90, US$3.20 and
US$5.50 per day (2011 PPP)

	$1.90	$3.20	$5.50
Cambodia	0.24	0.66	1.61
Lao PDR	1.37	3.44	2.75
Myanmar	0.09	1.51	3.40
Vietnam	0.20	0.60	1.00
Singapore	–	0.18	0.18
Indonesia	0.70	2.00	2.30
Malaysia	–	–	0.19
Philippines	0.70	2.40	2.50
Thailand	–	0.20	2.69

Source: Authors' calculations from Albert et al. (2020), based
on World Bank analysis, and using 2021 population figures.
Note that Singapore's total population shrank by some
4.5 per cent in 2020 and 2021, indicating migrant workers
being forced out of the city-state.

requirements on the banking sector. These were a major government expense,
accounting for some two-thirds of all spending on pandemic support packages
globally in 2020. In addition, most countries directed funding to health and income
support, in a range of measures including cash transfers, wage subsidies, tax
reductions and employment creation subsidies. Despite measures to cushion the
impact on the most vulnerable, estimates of the anticipated increase in poverty
during 2020 alone (Table 6) suggest that – at the US$3.20 a day poverty line – an
additional 2 per cent of Indonesia's population, and 2.4 per cent of the Philippines'
population, would have fallen into poverty.

Policy initiatives and fiscal capacity were more constricted in Southeast Asia
and, compared with other countries, total spending on Covid measures was low.
By the end of 2020, Japan had spent the equivalent of 66.6 per cent of GDP on
pandemic measures, two-thirds of it on health and income support. China spent
52 per cent of GDP, more than half of which was on health and income. The
equivalent figures for our case study countries (Table 7) show that Malaysia
spent significantly more in total than its neighbours, especially to stabilise its
economy, but also in direct health and income support (including its wage
subsidy programme). Thailand, with a lower overall spend, allocated over

Table 7 Components of Covid packages in Southeast Asia:
as % of GDP, to end 2020

	Malaysia	Thailand	Indonesia	Philippines
Economic/monetary measures	13.5	7.7	7.3	2.2
Health and income support	6.8	8.3	3.6	3.7
Other unspecified	2.5	0	0	0
Total	22.8	16.0	10.9	5.9

Source: ADB (2021).

8 per cent of GDP to health and income support. In Indonesia and the Philippines – with higher percentages of their population already near to poverty, and likely to have substantial 'new' poverty – the total spending, and that allocated to health and income support, were much lower (ADB 2021). Countries with the higher risk of poverty, but also with the lowest revenue base, lagged in their response during the first year of the pandemic.

It is clear much of this relatively limited new spending utilised already established channels. This makes obvious sense; if you have a distribution mechanism in place for providing income support to the poor, policy can simply increase the spending. In Indonesia, there was increased spending, and also a broadening of eligibility, for both the *PKH* CCT and the *Sembako* staple food programme; the latter was expanded to twenty million households. Somewhat later, Indonesia developed an additional Cash Social Assistance transfer for another nine million households not eligible for *PKH* or *Sembako*. In Thailand, emergency 'top-up' funding was added to the Child Support grant, and in July 2020 additional temporary increases for the Child Support Grant, Disability Grant, Old Age Allowance and the state welfare (food) card. In May 2020, the Philippines delivered major cash transfers, including the Social Amelioration Program, discussed below, to eighteen million low-income families for two months. Malaysia appears not to have focussed on cash transfers until September 2020 when it announced temporary increases to its *BSH* cash transfers, plus smaller grants to M40 (middle 40 per cent) households and singles. Then in 2021 there was a substantial increase in the *Bantuan Orang Tua* social pension, though it was still restricted to very small numbers of beneficiaries (World Bank 2020a).

Other examples of using existing administrative systems were reductions in compulsory social insurance contributions for both employers and employees, which occurred in both Thailand and Malaysia. In the latter country this has been used in the past as a fiscal policy measure to stimulate spending through what is, in effect, a temporary tax cut. Existing public work programmes were also utilised. The Philippines had a major emphasis on short-term employment creation, using an existing policy mechanism (TUPAD/DOLE), while Indonesia allocated existing Village Fund resources to cash-for-work programmes as well as for cash transfers at the discretion of local leaders. Indonesia also increased spending on its Pre-Employment programme, an existing system of online training with a small payment for the unemployed.

New initiatives were most prominent in Malaysia, where a large part of the pandemic response was directed to shoring up the position of businesses, cutting taxes and rents, and developing a major wage subsidy programme to prevent unemployment. From March 2020, firms with up to 200 employees that could demonstrate a decline in revenue received subsidies for three months to retain lower-income workers. That policy was then extended to the end of 2020, and again in early 2021, though now restricted to the tourism and retail sectors, in firms with up to 500 employees. Malaysia also developed multiple programmes to support small enterprises with tax reductions, grants to join the digital economy, micro-credit and rent reductions. Thailand developed a smaller wage subsidy system much later, in mid-2021, for firms with less than 200 employees. In August 2020, Indonesia initiated cash grants to unemployed workers who were enrolled in BPJS *Ketenagakerjaan*, the government agency established in 2014 as the successor to *Jamsostek*. It was called a 'wage subsidy', though it did not have the character of the Malaysian system, being more like a short-term unemployment benefit. In early 2021, Thailand did likewise, with a cash transfer to unemployed social insurance members, and extended it in mid-2021. In May 2021, Thailand experimented with a grant to the middle-class through a co-payment scheme to encourage their consumption spending, while in the same month, the Philippines – following criticism of how poorly its low-income cash transfers had been targeted – considered the idea of a universal cash grant regardless of income.

These initiatives present a complex picture, with multiple packages and an obvious air of urgency, and a common focus on using existing mechanisms; but several differences emerge. Malaysia gave major emphasis to supporting employers to ensure they kept their workers, and only came later to cash transfers. It was clear from early in the crisis that migrant workers in Malaysia (and Thailand) bore the brunt of sudden unemployment. The Malaysian Minister for Human Resources made it clear that if anyone was to be made redundant, migrant workers should go first; many did, and were not protected by any income support measures (ILO 2020). Indonesia's focus was income support spending, both to maintain consumption activity and to protect the poor, through additional cash into existing targeted systems. Thailand used existing income support measures for additional funding, mostly targeted but including the universal social pension, and only developed a partial wage subsidy programme. The Philippines had a major emphasis on work creation programmes, along with income support.

It is too early to know how well these countries' social protection systems have shielded the vulnerable. It will only be later that we can examine increases in poverty and gauge who has suffered most. But we can conjecture that Malaysia's wage subsidy and other measures have kept their relatively advanced capitalist system afloat, if at the expense of the underclass of migrant workers. Indonesia's long experience with targeting cash transfers, and the new spending sent down existing channels, may have provided some protection for the most vulnerable. By contrast, the efforts in Thailand and the Philippines look much less reassuring. The relatively high spending in Thailand on health and income support in Table 7 suggests the volume of redistribution may be significant, but much of it may have gone on the (nearly) universal Old Age Allowance, because even a small increase would be costly.

At the same time, there were criticisms of government failure, inept leadership and corruption in Indonesia, the Philippines and Thailand. The most spectacular example was the case of Indonesia's Minister of Social Affairs Juliari Batubara, the figure responsible for the *Sembako* staple food card. In December 2020, he was charged with taking bribes equivalent to US$2.3 million from vendors wanting contracts to supply food staples, while also embezzling US$1.02 million from the *Sembako* fund. When he was sentenced to twelve years in jail, a *Jakarta Post* editorial suggested he should have been considered for the death penalty (Editors 2021). Likewise, citizens' confidence in the Thai government was badly damaged by its handling of the pandemic, and in particular its choice to rely on the Sinovac vaccine, which was said to 'smell fishy' given a Thai conglomerate was a business partner in Sinovac (Pongsudhirak 2021). In the Philippines, a Senate enquiry into procurement of overpriced and poor quality personal protective equipment generated 'a nauseating stink, not just a whiff, of corruption' (Pascual 2021).

As to whether Covid responses in our four focus countries may signal significant change to their social protection systems, it is worth noting that almost all new initiatives had the character of one-off increases, some of which were then repeated. They appear to be temporary expedients rather than signalling major change. There are no obvious signs the pandemic has stimulated a rethink of social protection policies, though there have been some arguing a need for change. Nixon (2020), for instance, observed that 'Malaysia remains trapped in a low-tax, low welfare framework ... with a deeply diminished tax base, negligible transfer system and no permanent social protection programme'. Similarly, Williams (2021) argued that 'the COVID crisis has exposed huge gaps in Malaysia's social protection system', particularly with regard to pensions and the poor. There has been commentary in Thailand that the pandemic should lead to a welfare state, through 'more systematic social protection' and that this will require tax collection targeting inheritance, land and property (Thai PBS World 2021b). There has been some discussion about unemployment insurance, already implemented in Malaysia and now trialled in Indonesia and Thailand, though, as argued earlier, the social insurance model is of no benefit to informal workers.

In the longer term the experience of the pandemic may stimulate greater pressure for more comprehensive social protection systems, and governments may be willing, or find themselves compelled to act. But the shock of dealing with widespread dislocation, and presumably increases in poverty, may in the immediate future be balanced against the need to repair unprecedented budget deficits.

2.7 Summary and Conclusion

The evolution of social protection systems in our four focus countries began with social insurance for privileged groups, and with policies of FBE. Over time, these systems became more inclusive through the introduction of new social insurance, subsidised health care and social assistance targeted to the poor. However, there is significant unevenness across countries in the breadth and depth of social protection. Important gaps remain when systems are built on the insurance model, with its assumption of a formal work relationship of employer and wage. The adequacy and coverage of social assistance such as cash transfers and social pensions varies widely, and there have been serious problems with non-compliance and misallocation in some programmes. Government responses to Covid appear to have largely expanded existing programmes on a temporary basis with little evidence of a major shift towards institutionalisation of more progressive policies.

3 Theoretical Considerations

How should we understand this pattern of social protection development in our four focus countries? As noted earlier, our answer to this question emphasises the role of politics and power. In this section, we lay the basis for this analysis by examining existing approaches to understanding the politics of social protection in Southeast Asia and outlining an alternative approach based on political settlements analysis, a framework that emphasises the relative strength of competing political and social actors. Much work in comparative social policy has been concerned with the construction of typologies of social protection or welfare regimes (Abrahamson 2011). It is important to note that we are not engaging in this exercise. We are instead attempting to characterise the patterns of what has been developed and what is lacking and to explain these patterns in terms of the nature of political settlements. This approach goes beyond a classification exercise to explore how social protection systems express relationships of power and interest and how they change in response to shifts in these relationships. After outlining our theoretical approach, we turn to examining the political dynamics which have shaped the evolution of social protection systems in each of our four case countries.

3.1 Existing Approaches

In writing about social protection in Southeast Asian countries, scholars have focused on describing the nature of social protection policies, measuring levels and the distribution of social spending, assessing the impact of various schemes on poverty and inequality and evaluating the design of these schemes rather than analysing the politics of social protection (ADB 2019; Hardjono et al. 2010; UNESCAP and ILO 2021). In explaining the pattern of social protection development, they have accordingly tended to attribute this to proximate causes: levels and allocations of funding, the design and inclusiveness of programmes and levels of coordination in government management. To the extent that they *have* examined the politics of social protection, they have adopted one of three main alternative approaches.

The first has focused on the influence of cultural factors. Several scholars have argued that 'Confucian' values such as respect for education, filial piety, deference to authority and the relative importance of family and kinship ties have produced a strong emphasis on the role of families in providing social protection and a relatively limited role for the state, except in relation to education (Jones 1993). This concern with Confucian values reflects the prominence of Singapore as a focus in the literature on 'East Asian welfare regimes', the other foci being the Confucian 'tiger economies' of South Korea, Taiwan and Hong Kong (Peng and Wong 2010: 657–8). In a similar vein, Yuda (2020: 223) has suggested that social protection systems in Indonesia, Brunei and Malaysia can be understood in terms of an 'Islamic welfare ethics', whereby 'collective responsibility' is expressed in the obligation to donate part of wealth to the poor (*zakat*). Croissant (2004) has argued that such culturalist perspectives offer limited explanatory power because of Southeast Asia's diversity. Confucian values, for instance, might provide some insight into the evolution of social protection systems in Singapore and Vietnam, both of which have a significant Confucian heritage, but not in Indonesia, Brunei and Malaysia (which are predominantly Islamic), the Philippines and Timor Leste (which are predominantly Catholic), or Thailand, Myanmar, Cambodia and Lao PDR (which are predominantly Buddhist). At the same time, culturalist perspectives obscure how social protection systems embody particular political and social interests and are consequently subject to conflict and contestation. For this reason, and their emphasis on the enduring effects of cultural traits, they struggle to explain change in social protection systems.

The second approach proposes that social protection in Southeast Asia reflects the imperatives of late industrialisation and the presence of developmental states (Holliday 2000; Pierson 2005). The argument is that states have pursued a 'productivist' strategy of privileging economic over social policy, promoting industrial competitiveness and facilitating rapid economic growth rather than access to welfare. Governments have paid attention to formal sector workers but otherwise kept social expenditures at modest levels except, as Pierson (2005: 408) has noted, in 'an emphasis on the "investment" areas of education and health care'. In this respect, Southeast Asian states have followed the example set by late industrialising neighbours such as Japan, China, Korea and Taiwan, indicating the presence of a welfare model characteristic of East Asia as a whole (Gough 2001). But while 'productivism' helps explain the importance attached to formal private and public sector workers and education in Southeast Asia, it only explains the relative neglect of other areas by default. In addition, there is some ambiguity about what a developmental state looks like, given that regimes in Malaysia, Indonesia, Thailand and the Philippines have more commonly been described as oligarchic and predatory, rather than developmental (Rosser and van Diermen 2018). Finally, and most importantly for our purposes, the functionalist nature of the late industrialisation approach means that like the culturalist approach, it lacks a sense of how social protection systems embody particular political and social interests and are consequently subject to conflict and contestation. As such, it also struggles to explain change in social protection systems over time.

The third approach to examining the politics of social protection policy in Southeast Asia – in particular developments since the mid-1980s – focuses on the effects of democratic reform, especially in Indonesia, Thailand and the Philippines. Democratisation in these countries, it is argued, created an incentive for political leaders to champion social protection because such policies are popular with electorates and will help them win votes, or position themselves, or favoured successors, for re-election. At the same time, democratisation has opened up opportunities for progressive groups to participate more in advocacy and policymaking and advance the cause of social protection reform (Aspinall 2014; Haggard and Kaufman 2008). In some cases, this can be about using popular social protection policies to legitimise conservative and authoritarian leadership, rather than promote a progressive agenda, as Ramos (2020) suggests in an analysis of social policy in the Philippines under Rodrigo Duterte. She argues that democratic competition pushed Duterte to pursue social protection to build a stronger support base among the poor, in so doing creating a stronger political base for authoritarian change, though such reform could evolve in more progressive directions over time. In these ways, the democratisation explanation brings a dialectic component into the analysis that is missing in the culturalist and late industrialisation approaches. In focusing attention on the ways that a more democratic polity allows spaces for both old and new elites and interests to develop populist, and sometimes progressive, policies of social protection, it offers an important and insightful explanation of the political dynamics shaping social protection reform. Its weakness is that it does not account for what came before democratisation or resistance to progressive social protection reform that can occur in democratic political systems, both of which can shape the types of social protection that emerge in the wake of democratisation.

In sum, then, to better understand the pattern of social protection development in our four focus countries, we need a theoretical approach that gives regard to how social protection systems embody political and social interests and change over time in response to shifts in power relationships and processes of conflict and contestation. Further, this approach needs to not only account for how democratisation can create greater scope for progressive social protection reform by altering the balance of power between these interests, but also provide a context in which anti-reform interests mount resistance to change or harness it to authoritarian or conservative agendas.

3.2 A Political Settlements Approach

To address these matters, in this study we employ an analytical framework that sees social protection policy and its implementation as the product of a 'political settlement' (Lavers and Hickey 2016; Nino-Zarazua et al. 2012). Political settlements theorists contend that 'institutions' – that is, the rules, regulations and enforcement mechanisms governing economic and social activity (including social protection) – not only influence individual behaviour and determine macro-level development outcomes such as economic growth, but also shape how resources and opportunities are distributed within society. Further, they propose that institutions reflect relationships of power and interest, and that institutional change is a matter of political and social struggle. Consistent with this understanding, they define political settlements as 'the balance or distribution of power between contending social groups and social classes, on which any state is based' (Di John and Putzel 2009: 4). The implication is that institutions are subject to change over time as a result of shifts in the balance of power between competing actors and associated processes of conflict and contestation (Lavers and Hickey 2016).

In exploring the balance of power and contestation, political settlements theorists typically focus on elites – politicians, large capitalists, government technocrats, donors and predatory bureaucrats – because these are the most powerful groups in developing countries (Di John and Putzel 2009). They focus less on non-elite groups because such groups occupy a subordinate position in the power structure and cannot participate effectively in the construction of institutional arrangements. However, some recent contributions (Hickey et al. 2015; Rosser 2016) have sought to incorporate 'popular forces' – workers, peasants and NGO activists – into political settlements analysis, because they can play a significant role when empowered by democratic reform or structural change in the economy and society. At times, they can become party to the political settlements that determine the institutional arrangements governing economic and social activity. In this study, we adopt the latter approach because, as we will see, non-elite actors have at times played a crucial role in both promoting and resisting social protection changes in Southeast Asia.

Importantly, given our earlier discussion of the effects of democratisation, political settlements analysis recognises that political regimes matter due to the incentives they create for political leaders, and the opportunities they present for popular forces to organise and participate in policymaking. Ultimately, however, it emphasises the impact of the broader configuration of power and interest within which political regimes are situated, how this changes over time and how it shapes the purposes to which specific institutions are harnessed.

Operationalising the political settlements approach to study the politics of social protection means identifying the actors involved in contesting social protection policy and its implementation in specific contexts, and understanding how particular outcomes serve or harm their interests. It also entails understanding the evolution of social protection in terms of continuities and shifts in the balance of power between actors, and recognising that while all key actors may agree on some measures, they may disagree on the need for others, resulting in contestation. The implications are that the pattern of social protection institutions reflects the configuration of power and interest within society, and these institutions can change as a result of shifts in the balance of power between competing actors and processes of contestation. Broadly the framework suggests that social protection reform is least likely where political settlements are exclusionary and dominated by elites who have a vested interest in limiting investment in social protection schemes, particularly ones that benefit the poor and vulnerable. Conversely, social protection reform is more possible in contexts where political settlements are more inclusive – that is, subordinate groups are well organised and able to mount a challenge to elite rule. Given that democratisation opens up new opportunities for poor and marginalised elements to participate in policymaking, the latter circumstance is more likely to be the case under democratic or democratising regimes than authoritarian ones (Lavers and Hickey 2016; Nino-Zarazua et al. 2012).

Political settlements analysis has its origins in the study of economic growth in developing countries (Khan 2010), although over time it has been applied to a wider range of issues including social protection (Lavers and Hickey 2016; Nino-Zarazua et al. 2012). While it has distinctive origins, it is important to note that it has much in common with 'power resources' theory, the dominant approach to the study of comparative welfare regimes. The foundation stone in this line of work, Esping-Andersen's (1990) *The Three World of Welfare Capitalism*, advanced an influential typology of first world welfare states – as social democratic, liberal, or conservative – and sought to explain their emergence in terms of the 'power resources' of classes, interests and political actors (Korpi 2006 see also Gough 2001). In short, it argued that where labour unions were strong and political parties that represented them had enough time in office, countries could develop a more social democratic model of welfare, while strong conservative and familial forces, and Christian Democrats in office, resulted in a more conservative model of welfare (Arts and Gelissen 2010). Political settlements analysis shares with 'power resources' theory a common concern with how policy outcomes reflect the balance of power between different groups and how this balance changes over time. The main differences between the two approaches are that: (i) power resources theory has been used mainly to examine the emergence of welfare states in Europe and North America while political settlements analysis has been used mainly to analyse developing societies; and (ii) power resources theory is explicitly class-centric in orientation, focusing on trade unions and left-wing political parties as actors, while political settlements analysis is more eclectic in how it defines the main actors and interests, allowing its application to be tailored to a diversity of contexts.

In the following section, we start to apply the political settlements framework to our four focus countries by identifying the coalitions of actors who have contributed to the political settlements shaping social protection in these countries and identifying their respective interests and agendas.

4 Actors, Interests and Agendas

Broadly speaking, four main coalitions of actors have made up the political settlements that have shaped social protection in our four focus countries. We label these respectively predatory elements, technocratic elements, progressive elements and political entrepreneurs. It is important to note that this fourfold typology is a heuristic device rather than a rigid classification. While we identify particular individuals, groups and organisations as being associated with these coalitions and describe these coalitions as having distinct interests and agendas, in reality, the boundaries between them can be blurry and their memberships fluid, with particular individuals, groups and organisations sometimes moving between coalitions depending on their interests and agendas in relation to specific social protection issues. Nevertheless, we believe that the typology captures the main components in the political settlements that have shaped social protection systems in our four focus countries as well as the fault lines marking contestation between them.

The first coalition – predatory elements – includes the elites occupying the upper echelons of the state and controlling the commanding heights of the economy, a group often described as 'oligarchs' (Winters 2012). These figures have sought to exploit their positions and connections to generate rents for personal enrichment and to lubricate personal and political networks. They have recognised that state investment in social protection (especially education and, to some extent, health) is useful for promoting economic development – from which they benefit due to their economic position – through contributing to human resource development and political and social stability. But, otherwise, they have had little commitment to social protection programmes, preferring governments spend on areas such as infrastructure, industrial projects and subsidised credit programmes that are more central to their business activities. To the extent they have supported social protection initiatives, they have had an interest in ensuring these initiatives privilege lower-level military and bureaucratic officials and politicians – for instance, by providing them with pension benefits, opportunities for corruption or opportunities to fuel patronage networks and buy votes – as the price of their continuing political support (Ramesh and Asher 2000). This coalition of actors thus can also include lower-level officials involved in the implementation of social protection programmes such as local education or health officials, school principals and health facility heads, who engage in predatory behaviour (Widoyoko 2011).

The second coalition – technocratic elements – has consisted of liberal economic technocrats in government and their supporters within international financial institutions such as the World Bank and the International Monetary

Fund (IMF), bilateral donors and other bodies controlling mobile capital. This coalition has supported investment in social protection to ameliorate poverty, build human resources to contribute to productivity and economic development and manage the sometimes volatile politics of economic reforms such as reducing fuel subsidies (Moroz 2020; World Bank 2001). But it has insisted social protection programmes must be sustainable, affordable, cost-effective and based on evidence about what works and why (Rokx et al. 2009; World Bank 2014); it has also sought to promote the role of market forces and the private sector in the provision of social services (London 2018). Both positions have mitigated against support for increased state investment in social protection, with the result that technocratic elements have fluctuated between support for investment in social protection (for instance, when levels of investment have fallen below those required to reduce poverty, build required human resources and manage the politics of economic reform) and support for cuts to such investment (for instance, when countries have faced serious fiscal difficulties or sought to reduce perceived waste). The influence of this agenda has reflected structural pressures on governments due to their budget constraints, the power of mobile capital to relocate to alternate jurisdictions, technocrats' direct access to policymaking processes and the active promotion by powerful Western governments of a liberal economic agenda as part of efforts to contain communism during the Cold War and to promote the interests of Western business (Tadem 2020; Winters 1996).

The third coalition – progressive elements – has consisted of domestic and international NGOs, labour organisations, left-wing parties, academics, professional organisations and UN bodies such as the ILO and WHO that are committed to human rights, equity and social justice. This set of actors has promoted expanded and equitable access to social protection, seeing this as essential to combatting poverty and inequality (Gonzales and Manasan 2002; Kim 2015). It has accordingly called on governments to invest more in social protection benefitting the poor and vulnerable. At the same time, it has been critical of technocratic measures seeking to expand the role of market forces and the private sector in social services, viewing them as regressive. Members of this coalition have often lacked instrumental and structural leverage over the state (Quimpo 2020). But they have had some influence due to their ability – at least in democratic contexts – to access the media, mobilise popular support, compete in elections, hold demonstrations and make strategic use of court systems. In the case of UN agencies, they have also been able to operate through official channels (Kim 2015).

The fourth coalition has been political entrepreneurs at both the national and local levels running for, or occupying, executive offices in a context of democratic competition. Under more democratic conditions, both the old oli-garchic elites and sometimes more progressive groups have taken on roles as political entrepreneurs. Such figures have employed a variety of strategies, including (1) the cultivation of mafia-like networks through patronage distribu-tion; (2) the consolidation of party machines to enhance their institutional capacity and (3) the mobilisation of the poor through populist and redistributive policies (Rosser and Wilson 2012). These strategies are not mutually exclusive but come together in particular combinations varying from case to case. To the extent that political entrepreneurs have sought to mobilise the poor through populist and redistributive policies they have opened opportunities for social protection reforms even if they might be doing so to legitimise conservative and authoritarian rule rather than promote progressive politics (Ramos 2020). Because such figures have typically hailed from oligarchic or progressive camps, they also fit within the first and third groups above. We identify them separately here because of their distinctive interests and agendas and ability to influence policy and its implementation in democratic contexts.

In the following sections, we examine the balance of power between these elements – that is, the political settlement – in each of our four focus countries and how this has changed over time. We also examine how this changing balance of power has shaped the nature of social protection policy and its implementation, focusing in each country on two illustrative cases drawn from the sectors of education, health coverage and income support.

In these sections, we argue that our four focus countries have been character-ised in recent decades by the continued dominance of predatory elements – especially oligarchic elites – and the relative weakness of progressive actors. Technocratic elements have also been important, but their influence has varied between countries and over time. Oligarchic dominance has had distinctive origins and characteristics in each case but, once established, has endured notwithstanding democratic reforms and economic and social crises. Democratic reforms have facilitated more inclusive political settlements, creat-ing electoral incentives for politicians to introduce social protection reforms and opening up greater opportunities for progressive actors such as civil society activists to participate in policymaking. Economic and social crises have also generally enhanced the position of progressive elements as well as that of technocratic elements. The ruptures of the AEC and the pandemic, for instance, tilted the balance of power in their favour by shining a light on gaps in social protection systems, precipitating new mobilisations and compelling govern-ments to seek support from donors. At the same time, though, powerful politico-business oligarchies have retained their dominance in all four cases due to their ability to accumulate and concentrate wealth, capture democratic institutions and fend off protests and challenges through intimidation and repression. The result – in line with the expectations of the political settlements framework as noted above – has been a political context making significant progressive social protection reform possible, while at the same time ensuring social protection systems in the region remain incomplete and often inadequate.

5 Indonesia

5.1 The Political Settlement

In recent decades, predatory elements and, to a lesser extent, technocratic elements have been the dominant elements in Indonesia's political settlement while progressive elements have been relatively marginalised. This configuration of power and interest was founded early in the 'New Order' period (1966–8). After seizing power in a 1965 coup, the Indonesian military emasculated the political parties and the national parliament, seized control of the bureaucracy and subordinated the judiciary to political and bureaucratic authority. With control over the state apparatus, and in the absence of significant checks and balances, New Order officials engaged in extensive predatory activity, enriching themselves and building political and patronage networks. They cultivated powerful private business conglomerates that controlled large parts of the Indonesian economy through privileged access to state subsidies, licences, facilities and concessions (Robison 1986; Rosser 2002). This provided the context for the emergence of a set of powerful politico-business families headed by senior New Order officials and/or their business clients (Robison and Hadiz 2004).

At the same time, the New Order granted considerable authority over economic and social policy to a group of technocratic officials known as the 'Berkeley Mafia', who collaborated with the World Bank and the IMF, especially at times of economic crisis. With their assistance, the government introduced economic policy reforms that served to attract mobile domestic and foreign capital, restore economic stability in the wake of crises and keep the country on a path of economic growth (Robison 1986; Winters 1996). The technocrats were, however, severely constrained by the fact that predatory elements dominated the political system. In implementing reforms, they often provided new opportunities for politically connected conglomerates while ensuring that the latter's core business interests and associated rents remained protected (Rosser 2002).

By contrast, progressive elements were prevented from exercising much influence during the New Order period by the imposition of authoritarian controls. Most notably, the New Order banned the Indonesian Communist

Party – which had been among Asia's largest communist parties – and in 1965–6 the regime oversaw the killing of as many as one million suspected communists. It also established a corporatist system of interest group representation that constrained independent organisation by groups such as labour, the peasantry and professionals. Many of these groups became formally incorporated into Golkar, the New Order's electoral vehicle. Finally, while the New Order permitted NGOs, they were severely restricted in their ability to advocate for progressive causes through controls over freedom of expression, freedom of organisation and judicial independence (Robison 1986; Rosser 2002).

The onset of the AEC, the fall of President Suharto and the transition to a more democratic political system in the late 1990s tilted the balance of power away from predatory elements in favour of technocratic and progressive elements. Widespread corporate bankruptcies undermined the economic base of the oligarchic elite, and increased mobilisation by students, workers and NGOs calling for change, undermined their control over the political and social order. At the same time, the crisis enhanced the influence of technocratic elements by forcing the government to negotiate a rescue package with the IMF. Democratic reform contributed further to a shift in power towards progressive elements by creating electoral incentives for political leaders to introduce redistributive policies and by opening up opportunities for NGOs and other progressive elements to participate in policymaking, with the national parliament, the courts and the media being particularly important in this respect (Rosser et al. 2005). But, despite these changes, predatory oligarchic elites retained their political dominance, adjusting to the more democratic environment by forging new alliances and using political parties to capture the state apparatus at both the national and local levels (Robison and Hadiz 2004). Their continued dominance was best illustrated by the fact that many of the political figures who contested presidential elections in the post–New Order period – B. J. Habibie, Susilo Bambang Yudhoyono, Wiranto, Prabowo Subianto and Jusuf Kalla – had held senior political positions, held senior military positions and/or built business empires under the New Order.

The Covid pandemic did little, if anything, to alter this situation. Like the AEC, the associated economic and social crisis precipitated a shift in power away from predatory elements towards technocratic and progressive elements by causing a severe social crisis, highlighting gaps in existing social protection policies, sparking renewed activism by progressive elements and forcing the government to borrow new funds from international donors. But this was not sufficient to fundamentally alter the balance of power, nor even to reconfigure it to the same extent as occurred in the late 1990s. The Joko Widodo (Jokowi) administration (2014–present) remained in office and dominated by predatory oligarchic figures with backgrounds in the military, bureaucracy and major political parties. No obvious challenger to his government emerged.

Indeed, some have argued that the pandemic led to a reassertion of predatory dominance over Indonesian politics and increasing exclusion of progressive elements. Mietzner (2020), for instance, noted that the Indonesian government's response to Covid was accompanied by moves to silence criticism of Jokowi and, in particular, his government's handling of the pandemic. Similarly, Setijadi (2021: 297) has argued that 'under the guise of promoting social and political stability in the time of Covid, Jokowi has also allowed for further democratic regression in Indonesia through laws that restrict freedom of speech and through the further empowerment of the military and intelligence agencies in civilian life'.

5.2 Free Basic Education

The New Order officially abolished user fees at government primary schools in 1977 and at government junior secondary schools in 1994, as noted earlier. However, Indonesian schools were permitted to charge fees for a wide range of services, products and activities, while illegal fees were also widespread. This situation reflected the contradictory interests of dominant predatory elements. On the one hand, they saw education as developing the human resources required to drive economic growth, and as a mechanism through which they could exert political control, mobilise political support and achieve nation-building objectives. But on the other, they used educational institutions as a vehicle for generating rents and distributing patronage resources. This situation also reflected technocratic concerns about the level of government spending on education particularly during the fiscal crisis caused by the collapse of international oil prices in the mid-1980s. The New Order had invested heavily in the 1970s and early 1980s in expanding the school system when its coffers were full with petrodollars. But it cut education spending significantly following the collapse of international oil prices, leaving many schools bereft of funds (Rosser and Fahmi 2016; Rosser and Joshi 2013).

When the New Order collapsed in 1998, there was broad agreement among technocratic and progressive elements that the government needed to do more to realise FBE including by increasing government spending on education. For instance, the World Bank (1998) encouraged the government to reduce the cost of junior secondary education for poor students, suggesting scholarships and direct provision of funds to schools as solutions. The notion of FBE also fits well with the desire of progressive groups to promote equitable access to education through a well-funded public school system. In the case of populist political entrepreneurs at the local and national levels, it also fits well with their agenda of mobilising votes in elections given the apparent widespread popularity of the policy among voters.

In this context, post–New Order governments introduced a series of legislative changes, including amendments to the 1945 Constitution, that provided FBE with a stronger legal basis. At the same time, various local leaders promoted FBE within their respective regions, seeing the policy as a vote-winner (Rosser and Sulistiyanto 2013). In 2005, the Yudhoyono government provided FBE with stronger financial foundations by introducing the School Operational Assistance (BOS) programme, which provides funding to government and private primary and junior secondary schools to cover 'operational' costs, in exchange for them eliminating or reducing their fees. It also enacted a teacher certification programme, one effect of which was to increase teachers' salaries, potentially reducing their propensity to demand informal payments. Finally, President Yudhoyono actively encouraged local governments to implement FBE and in the run-up to the 2009 presidential election launched a public information campaign to promote awareness of the new FBE policy. This involved blanket advertising across all forms of media – newspapers, television, radio and the internet (Rosser and Joshi 2013).

However, translating FBE into practice proved difficult. First, there was resistance from some predatory elements within the education bureaucracy, in particular at the school and local education agency levels, who sought to maintain school fees – for instance, in the guise of 'voluntary' contributions – to generate extra income for teachers, principals and local bureaucrats. Second, technocratic elements within the central government and their supporters in the business community expressed concern about the cost of FBE, especially if extended to all public school students (not just the poor) and accompanied by pay increases for teachers. Finally, the very principle of FBE was contested in some regions. While many district governments – which have primary responsibility for education policy under the country's decentralisation laws – and provincial governments supported FBE, and in a few cases even extended it to include the years of senior secondary school, others opposed it on the grounds that local residents were willing to pay fees for higher-quality education services and/or that their regions had other budgetary priorities. The result was uneven implementation of the policy in practice, undermining the level of social protection provided to the poor and marginalised (Rosser and Joshi 2013; Rosser and Sulistiyanto 2013).

The pandemic saw widespread school closures in Indonesia and a shift towards remote learning. But while remote learning was viable for students from higher socio-economic backgrounds, it was much less viable for the poor.

Only 40 per cent of Indonesians have internet access, primarily in cities; of 179,000 schools across the country, 18.4 per cent had electricity but no internet, and another 4.2 per cent had neither electricity nor internet (Harson 2020). There was widespread concern that 'learning inequalities' would widen further due to the pandemic (Yarrow and Afkar 2021). In an attempt to get students back to school in late 2021 some local governments introduced initiatives to assist children affected by the pandemic by, for instance, providing free school uniforms. But the pandemic also saw a continuation of school-level corruption, albeit at a much lower level (Sjafrina and Anggraeni 2021), suggesting illegal fees will be an enduring barrier to educational equity.

5.3 Health Coverage

Under the New Order, Indonesia provided health insurance to civil servants, military officials and veterans, as well as to those formal sector workers enrolled in social insurance. But it provided little, if any, coverage to other Indonesians, leaving them exposed to potentially catastrophic out-of-pocket health costs when ill. This approach was consistent with the interests of dominant predatory elements in directing state resources towards areas such as infrastructure and business subsidies that served their business activities, while privileging constituencies crucial to the New Order's continued rule. It also reflected technocratic concerns about the costs of healthcare that paralleled those related to education. The New Order made substantial investments in public primary health facilities, the recruitment of new health workers and a range of other health initiatives during the oil boom years. But it wound spending back following the collapse of international oil prices in the early- to mid-1980s. In this context, free universal health care was politically inconceivable. In 1994, the New Order introduced a health card that exempted poor families from health fees at public health facilities for a range of services. But it did not provide additional resources to fund local governments or public health facilities, and consequently the scheme was not implemented in many regions (Rosser 2012).

The reconfiguration of Indonesia's political settlement during and after the AEC provided the political basis for change. First, technocratic elements exploited the crisis to argue that the government needed to provide better and more equitable health coverage, although – echoing earlier concerns – they also worried about the fiscal sustainability of improved coverage (Rokx et al. 2009; World Bank 2000). Second, progressive public health experts and NGO activists pushed for expanded health coverage through advocacy, research and engagement work as well as lobbying and strategic litigation (Rosser 2017). Third, local and national politicians, running for or occupying executive offices, began to promote new health insurance schemes as part of their campaign strategies, given such schemes proved popular with the public, including the poor (Aspinall 2014; Pisani et al. 2017). Finally, the most important of these schemes – the JKN introduced in 2014 – drew crucial support from sections of the trade union movement. When the government delayed implementing legislation, thousands of labour activists held demonstrations across the country in 2010–11 calling for the enactment of the bill. Combined with a series of strategic court cases, these demonstrations put enormous pressure on the government to pass the legislation (Rosser 2017).

This proposed change in direction posed a significant threat to predatory elements. To free up funds for the new health insurance scheme the government had to cut fuel subsidies that primarily benefitted business and the middle class. The creation of the JKN – and the accompanying social insurance reforms related to labour such as pension savings and workplace injury insurance – meant increased costs for business due to mandatory social insurance charges (Pisani et al. 2017). It also entailed the transfer of control over existing health insurance funds from two social security SOEs – PT *Askes* and PT *Jamsostek* – to a new agency, BPJS *Kesehatan*. These SOEs were a source of funding for strategic government initiatives and rents for government officials, well-connected business groups and senior SOE officials. The result was a series of protests from the business community – or instigated by it – and from the traditional SOEs (especially *Jamsostek*) against cuts to fuel subsidies and against the implementing legislation for the JKN (van Diermen 2017).

In the end, such protests were unable to stop the legislation, reflecting the broad nature of the coalition formed in support of the new health insurance programme. But they did delay the JKN's introduction and send a clear signal to the country's political elites that future attempts to expand the scheme at the expense of the business community would be fiercely contested. Combined with enduring technocratic concerns about the fiscal sustainability of the JKN (Prabhakaran et al. 2019), this has constrained the government's ability to expand coverage to the whole population, notwithstanding its ambition of providing UHC.

From 2014, all the existing health insurance schemes – civil servants' insurance, formal sector cover under *Jamsostek*, and the national *Jamkesmas* and provincial *Jamkesda* schemes – were rolled into BPJS *Kesehatan*, with the stated aim of UHC (Murphy 2019). Membership of BPJS *Kesehatan* grew rapidly after 2014 until the pandemic, which produced an initial fall in membership followed by a modest recovery in 2021. As of June 2022, 39.4 per cent of the population was 'subsidised' by the central government (i.e. the poor receiving free coverage), and another 13.6 per cent was subsidised by provincial governments. Combined with existing contributors, a total of almost 88 per cent of the Indonesian population was now covered. But while this was an enormous achievement, there remained a 'missing middle' of 12.2 per cent (some thirty-four million people) who were without health insurance because they were not poor enough for 'subsidised' insurance, were not part of employment-based social insurance schemes or had not paid for their own insurance (databoks/katadata.co.id; accessed October 2022).

6 The Philippines

6.1 The Political Settlement

The Philippines' political settlement has also been characterised by the dominance of predatory politico-business families and, to a lesser extent, technocratic elements and the relative marginalisation of progressive elements; but its history and characteristics have been distinct. The Philippine oligarchy emerged during the colonial period, gaining control over land and early representative political institutions. Oligarchic families ruled, more or less uncontested, until 1972 when then-President Ferdinand Marcos declared martial law. He launched an attack on sections of the oligarchy considered a threat to his rule. However, as Anderson (1988: 22) observed, 'oligarchs who bent with the wind and eschewed politics for the pursuit of gain were mostly left undisturbed'. At the same time, Marcos used his authority to cultivate new oligarchs, including relatives, associates and senior military and bureaucratic officials.

The fall of the Marcos regime in 1986 amidst the emergence of a 'people power' movement, and subsequent transition to a more democratic system, saw the old oligarchy resume control over the state apparatus and the economy. The following decades witnessed the election of multiple presidents from the old families or closely aligned with them: Cory Aquino (1986–92), Fidel Ramos (1992–8), Gloria Macapagal Arroyo (2001–10) and Benigno Aquino III (2010–16). Although Marcos died in exile (1989), his wife and children returned to the Philippines and, along with various cronies and offsiders, soon became players again in politics (Winters 2012). In May 2022, Marcos' son, Ferdinand 'Bongbong' Marcos Jr, was elected president.

As in Indonesia, technocratic officials who collaborated with the World Bank and the IMF were allowed significant authority over economic and social policy, although arguably with less consistent influence than in Indonesia. After independence, the United States cultivated a small group of technocrats, offering bright youngsters opportunities to study in the United States and, in so doing, imbuing them with a commitment to free market capitalism. They became a key pillar of the Marcos regime, although their efforts to promote reform were often frustrated by Marcos' kleptocratic behaviour (Tadem 2014). Following the fall of Marcos, technocratic officials and their international donor backers continued to maintain some influence over government policy, reflecting the country's continued dependence on foreign aid and foreign investment, and desire to maintain good relations with the United States. But this influence has fluctuated significantly from administration to administration, and, as in the Marcos period, their efforts to promote reform have often been undermined by elite predation and corruption (Tadem 2018; Thompson 2010).

For their part, progressive forces have been a subordinate element in the country's political settlement, although, as in Indonesia, their influence has fluctuated over time. In contrast to communist parties in our other focus countries, the Communist Party of the Philippines (CPP) survived the period from the 1960s to the 1980s and emerged as a key source of opposition to the Marcos regime. However, its position as an opposition force – and one actively engaged in guerrilla warfare – meant it had little influence within government. Its position has declined in the post-Marcos years, due largely to its non-participation in the 1986 people power movement, even though the CPP has competed in national elections for tactical reasons (Quimpo 2020). Other progressive elements – most notably NGOs – have fared better. Under Marcos, they had little influence within government because they were a key part of the political opposition, but the fall of Marcos opened new opportunities for progressive elements to influence and cooperate with the state; as Quimpo (2005: 248) has observed, democratisation provided increased 'opportunity for subordinate classes and communities to push for popular empowerment and, further, for a more equitable distribution of the country's wealth and ultimately to bring about a stable, more participatory and egalitarian democracy'.

At the same time, democratisation created incentives for politicians and political parties to promote pro-poor policies with electoral appeal. This dynamic was particularly strong under populist leaders such as Joseph Estrada (president from 1998 to 2001) and Rodrigo Duterte (2016–22) but has also characterised the presidencies of leaders with stronger oligarchic connections. Progressive elements have nevertheless remained in a subordinate position vis-à-vis the oligarchy despite these broad changes in the political environment – indeed, some analysts argue NGOs' increased engagement with the state in the post-Marcos era has merely led to their co-option by the dominant political and social forces (Reid 2008).

The AEC tilted the balance of power slightly in favour of technocratic and progressive elements. Although the economic and social effects of the AEC were less severe in the Philippines than Indonesia, the crisis still caused considerable economic and social disruption, triggered calls for social protection reform and forced the government to negotiate new forms of financial support from donors (Valenzuela 2000; World Bank 1999). At the same time, it also fuelled the popularity of Estrada, a political entrepreneur whose populist style of politics promised a better deal for the poor and marginalised, including in the form of social policy measures (Haggard 2008). But, as in Indonesia, these developments produced more a partial shift than a radical change in the country's political settlement. In office, Estrada did little for the poor, and he was ousted from office after three years in the wake of corruption allegations. This brought Gloria Macapagal Arroyo to power. The daughter of a former president, her presidency marked a return to oligarchic rule.

Covid had a similar effect. The pandemic caused even greater economic and social disruption than the AEC, saw progressive and technocratic elements advocate for further social protection reform, and forced the government to borrow from donors to support social protection initiatives (UNESCAP and ILO 2021; World Bank 2021). But ultimately the oligarchy remained firmly in control. Duterte had come to office in 2016 promising to challenge the power of the oligarchs, but in office, as with Marcos, he focused more on cultivating new oligarchs linked personally to him – widely termed 'Dutertegarchs' – and repressing civil society activists and journalists who criticised his rule. He did not change tack during the pandemic. Indeed, as in Indonesia, the pandemic saw moves to crack down on dissent and political opposition while the wealth of the country's richest grew (Auethavornpipat and Tanyag 2021).

6.2 Income Support

During the Marcos and early post-Marcos years, the Philippine government provided little by way of income support to the poor. According to Pernia and Knowles (1998), it administered a cash transfer scheme targeting the poor in the late 1990s, but this was tiny. It was only towards the end of the 2000s that the government started to develop significant income support policies. Initially, the Arroyo government launched a pilot cash transfer project in 2007. Within a matter of months, it scaled up this project into a major CCT programme (*Pantawid Pamilyang Pilipino Program* or Bridging Program for the Filipino Family). Designed and partly funded by the World Bank, it targeted poor families with children, and/or pregnant mothers, providing monthly cash payments which varied with the number of children. The conditions include health centre visits, school attendance, prenatal consultations for pregnant women and participation in 'family development' and 'responsible parenthood' sessions (World Bank 2018a: 47). According to Dadap-Cantal et al. (2021: 372), Arroyo's decision to scale up the pilot was 'prompted by the food and fuel crisis in 2008, as well as the country's dismal performance in meeting the poverty targets of the Millennium Development Goals'.

The programme's growth thereafter was driven in no small part by the dynamics of electoral competition. Arroyo's successor, Benigno Aquino III, was elected in 2010 promising a new 'social contract' with the people. He had committed to 'an expanded conditional cash transfer programme by increasing the coverage' of *Pantawid* (*Business World* 2010). In office, the Aquino government increased the number of beneficiaries by more than one million, despite the reservations of the World Bank and the ADB. In 2012, automatic health insurance was included for *Pantawid* beneficiaries, and in 2013, the upper age limit for eligible children was increased from fourteen to eighteen. Aquino also developed, in 2012, a Modified CCT programme, targeting benefits to homeless and indigenous families. The same politics of political entrepreneurship continued under Duterte, who campaigned on a promise to fold a subsidised rice programme into *Pantawid* benefits (Dadap-Cantal et al. 2021). By 2017, the programme was enormous, costing 86.9 billion pesos, or 3.9 per cent of the total budget, dwarfing any other social protection measures. In 2018, it covered over 4.4 million households. In 2019, Duterte passed legislation institutionalising *Pantawid* as a permanent feature of social protection.

In a 2018 review, the World Bank described *Pantawid* as 'the Philippines' flagship national social protection program', and claimed that it was improving the resources and 'productivity' of poor households, investing in 'human capital', especially children 'to break the cycle of inter-generational poverty'. It also judged targeting to be 'successful', claiming that *Pantawid* is 'among the world's best programs in terms of successfully targeting the poor' (World Bank 2018a: 46, 48).

Another important income support programme, the Social Pension, was initiated in 2011, also positioned by Aquino as part of the commitment to a new social contract. At first, this was restricted to the 'indigent and infirm' aged eighty and over, with no family support and no other form of pension. Over five years, the Social Pension then expanded rapidly, as the age of eligibility was progressively dropped; by 2016 it was available to all aged sixty and over (Sicat and Mariano 2021). By 2017, the programme reached 2.6 million elderly and 'indigent' people, with a total budget commitment of 15 billion Pesos – equivalent to US$300 million (Velarde and Albert 2018; World Bank 2018a).

The Social Pension has, however, been undermined by predatory elements capturing programme benefits at the expense of the poor. Initially, the *Listahanan*, the register employed by *Pantawid*, was used to identify beneficiaries. But from 2014 the register was abandoned and the major part of eligibility decisions were devolved to local governments. As the programme

Table 8 Distribution of Pantawid and the social pension in the Philippines: Per cent of beneficiaries by income quintile (equal sized fifths of the population) 2017

	Q1 (poorest)	Q2	Q3	Q4	Q5 (richest)
Pantawid CCT	41.6	31.7	18.2	7.2	1.3
Social Pension (SocPen)	18.4	22.2	24.1	19.9	15.4

Source: World Bank 2018a: Table III.2, 30.

expanded, targeting was badly compromised. A process of validation through public exposure of draft eligibility lists ran into local patron–client networks. Velarde and Albert (2018: 11) reported that this had 'materially reduced' its equity of distribution; they quoted interviewees who had missed out, who spoke of needing to have 'strong connections' and who noted that 'the final decision is with the *barangay* [neighbourhood or village] captain. If you are an opponent of the *barangay* captain you really can't do anything about it'. Patronage networks distorting decisions on eligibility had led to local 'elite capture'. The result in distorted targeting can be seen in Table 8; the social pension was spectacularly misallocated, with over 35 per cent of beneficiaries being in the richest two-fifths of the population.

Similar problems afflicted a key income support part of the government's response to Covid. In March 2020, the Philippine government introduced a massive new cash transfer called the Social Amelioration Program (SAP). Unprecedented in scale, it provided payments to approximately eighteen million households, around 70 per cent of the population, including those covered by *Pantawid*. The payments were roughly equivalent to the monthly minimum wage and households' subsistence expenditures in each region (Cho et al. 2020). From the outset, the scheme was plagued by complaints of administrative corruption among local officials, forcing Duterte to announce a nationwide investigation. In one incident, 'a municipal official was caught on video telling aid recipients of a town near Manila that they would only receive half of the aid, while the other half of the money would be redistributed to those not listed for state help' (Gagne-Acoulon 2020).

6.3 Free Basic Education

Free basic education has a long history in the Philippines. The American colonial authorities established a free public school system underpinned by a Constitutional guarantee for free compulsory education (Schweisfurth et al. 2016) and subsequent Filipino Constitutions in 1935, 1943 and 1973 provided for free and compulsory education at least at the elementary level. Yet, in practice, schooling was far from free in the initial decades after independence and during the Marcos years. A World Bank analysis of 1986 data found that while public elementary schools did not charge tuition fees, public secondary schools did, with fees accounting for 9–10 per cent of operating cost per student (1988b: 27, 31). Both elementary and secondary public schools relied heavily on parent–teacher associations to raise funds for basic supplies, imposing additional costs on parents (World Bank 1988a: 70). Combined with other costs (transport, uniforms and textbooks) and overcrowding, poor quality education and widespread teacher absenteeism in public schools, the result was large numbers of children dropping out of public schools. Middle-class parents typically avoided public schools, enrolling their children in fee-charging, private schools (Fineman 1987).

The proximate cause of this situation was underfunding of the public education system, especially during the Marcos years. Education spending fell from 33 per cent of the national budget in 1966, to 13 per cent in 1978, placing enormous financial pressure on the public school system (Cortes 1980). This underfunding in turn reflected the oligarchic nature of the Philippines' political settlement. Government spending shifted away from education to defence and industry, and to free up funding for Marcos' pet projects. As Ansell (2010: 77–8) observed, this allocation 'reflected the educational spending preferences of his elite client base', especially the military and his cronies.

The fall of the Marcos regime saw progressive elements call for free and quality education as part of wider reforms aimed at effecting a transition to democratic rule based on principles of social justice (Lane 1990). In particular, they called on the government to eliminate voluntary and mandatory fees and increase spending on public education (Asia-South Pacific Education Watch 2007). The country's new political leadership championed FBE, seeing it as a way of building popular support for the new regime (Miller 1986).

By contrast, technocratic elements, led by the World Bank, pushed for an enhanced role in the education sector for private business, calling on the government to scale up Education Service Contracting (ESC), a scheme under which the government pays private schools to enrol students who cannot be accommodated within the public system (San Juan 2016; World Bank 1988a). For their part, predatory oligarchic elements sought to exploit the new business opportunities presented by ESC and attendant programmes (Riep 2015).

The outcome of this contest was a mix of policies and practices that simultaneously promoted FBE and undermined it. On the former side, initiatives included:

1) Constitutional amendments in 1987 obliging government to: 'protect and promote the right of all citizens to quality education at all levels', 'take appropriate steps to make such education accessible to all', 'establish and maintain a free public education in the elementary and high school levels' and 'assign the highest budgetary priority to education';

2) new legislation providing for free public secondary education (1988), for a free year of kindergarten (2012), and for two additional years of free secondary education (2013);

3) large increases in government spending on education, especially immediately following Marcos' ouster and the period since 2008 (Ansell 2010; World Bank 2020b); and

4) regular Department of Education directives since at least 2001 prohibiting schools from collecting fees and contributions during the enrolment period (USAID et al. 2007).

On the other side of the ledger, other policies dramatically expanded government funding of private schools through ESC. These included: enactment of the Government Assistance to Students and Teachers in Private Education (GASTPE) law in 1989, expansion of the GASTPE programme in 1998, and introduction of an Education Voucher System in 2006. By 2014, according to Riep (2015: 9) 'approximately 800,000 or nearly 60% of the 1.3 million students in private high schools were beneficiaries of ESC and GASTPE'. Schools participating in ESC/GASTPE were permitted to charge 'top-up' fees, undermining FBE and effectively excluding the poor from attending such schools (Civil Society Network for Education Reforms et al. 2016: 20).

The contest over FBE has also seen continued efforts by some public schools to raise funds from parents and students in breach of the 'no collections policy' through 'voluntary' contributions and outright extortion. In its 2020 Global Corruption Barometer, Transparency International (2020: 49) found that 18 per cent of Filipinos had paid a bribe for services at public schools in the previous twelve months. This contest has also seen continued underfunding of the public education system, notwithstanding increases in government education spending in recent years. Progressive elements not surprisingly believe the right to FBE in the Philippines continues to be widely breached. They have called on the government to increase spending, end the 'privatisation' and 'commercialisation' of education represented by the ESC and GASTPE, and take action to reduce the imposition of formal and informal fees (Asia-South Pacific Education Watch 2007: 17, 19–21; Civil Society Network for Education Reforms et al. 2016: 34).

As in Indonesia, Covid has caused widespread school closures, a shift towards remote learning and concerns about rising educational inequality due to inequitable internet access. It has also seen more than 2.7 million children drop out of school for economic reasons (Villegas 2021). However, by the end of 2021, the government had introduced no new measures related to access to education, according to the ILO's Social Protection Monitor. Progressive teacher organisations such as the Alliance of Concerned Teachers have condemned the government for its 'failure' to ensure the needs of poor and marginalised children are met during the pandemic and called for a return to in-class learning as early as possible (Perez-Rubio 2020).

7 Thailand

7.1 The Political Settlement

Predatory elements – in particular, an oligarchic elite fusing political power with massive wealth – have been the dominant element in Thailand's political settlement. As in Indonesia and the Philippines, they have maintained their dominance notwithstanding changes in political regime and crises such as the AEC and the pandemic. In contrast to both Indonesia and the Philippines, the oligarchy has its roots in Thailand's long period of absolutist rule, which ended in 1932 when a military coup forced the king to adopt a form of constitutional monarchy. But, as Phongpaichit and Baker (2016: 20) explain, the elite has been reconstituted over time in response to economic and political changes:

> Under the absolute monarchy, a bureaucratic elite developed from the late 19th century, and became entrenched in the public services. From the 1930s to the 1980s, the military high command dominated politics, and developed a belief in its right to rule. As the urban economy grew in the post-war era of development, new business groups grew powerful through their command of wealth, and demanded access to power through connections and through parliamentary politics. As prosperity spread upcountry, and better communications tied the provincial areas more tightly to the capital, a provincial business elite emerged and demanded a share of power. More recently, the senior judiciary and parts of civil society have also become important.

Although no longer an absolutist ruler, the Thai king and his family occupy the foremost position among the country's most powerful families and continue to hold the greatest wealth (Rhoden 2015).

Technocratic influence has provided some counterweight to oligarchic rule, waxing and waning over time. Technocratic officials exercised significant influence between 1976 and 1992 under military rule, as the domestic economy became more complex, 'and the world economy became a source of destabilizing shocks after the end of the Bretton Woods era' (Phongpaichit and Baker

2014: 284). But their influence fell significantly during the period of multi-party democracy from 1992 to 2006 as politicians and business assumed control over the state at the expense of military and bureaucratic elites. The period of the AEC was an important exception in this respect, seeing the country submit to an IMF rescue package. The election of businessman-turned-politician Thaksin Shinawatra in 2001 saw the technocrats marginalised again, as politicians and businesspeople resumed control (Phongpaichit and Baker 2014).

Their influence remained modest for much of the period thereafter, notwithstanding the fact that the military returned to power, initially on a short-term basis in the 2006 coup, and then on a longer-term basis after the next coup in 2014 (Pongsudhirak 2015, 2020). Internal party machinations saw the technocratic camp within the ruling *Palang Pancharat* party pushed aside in favour of politicians in a reshuffle early in the pandemic. But the Covid crisis did provide some new opportunities for technocratic influence as the government grappled with the economic and social effects of the pandemic and looked to technocratic officials and international donors to assist. For instance, the former were given a leading role in the Centre for Covid-19 Situation Administration, the government's main body for managing the pandemic (Ganjanakhundee 2021).

For their part, progressive elements have been largely marginalised, although less so during periods of democratic rule and moments of crisis, as in Indonesia and the Philippines. The Communist Party of Thailand's rural insurgency collapsed in the late 1970s with a mass defection of party activists. As Anderson (1990: 44) noted, that 'redounded principally to the benefit of the new Thai bourgeoisie. After 1978–9, it faced no serious threats from the left, or from below'. Progressive elements in NGOs and other sections of civil society were severely constrained in their ability to influence policy under military rule due to a range of authoritarian controls, but they successfully exploited the available democratic spaces. Hewison and Rodan (1994: 256–7) note that NGOs played 'leading and co-ordinating roles in the events of 1991 and 1992 which eventually led to the demise of a military government'. The onset of the AEC – which had a severe impact and exposed weaknesses in the country's system of social protection – and the emergence of a more populist style of politics under Thaksin created some opportunities for progressive elements to contribute to policymaking, particularly in health policy (see below), during the period between the AEC and Thaksin's ouster in 2006.

The conflict that emerged between Thaksin and his opponents – which led to him being overthrown in 2006 – involved, on one side, newer oligarchs (specifically Thaksin himself), progressive bureaucrats and some civil society and democracy activists and, on the other side, an alliance of the military, royalists, some of the middle-class, the Democrat party and much of the conservative bureaucracy (Hewison 2010). The latter alliance resented and feared Thaksin's popularity among the rural poor, whose votes they saw as being bought with populist policies of free health care, village funds and a farmer debt moratorium. As Hewison (2010: 131) explained: 'not only was Thaksin a strong and brash prime minister, but his party's new social contract unleashed the "masses" who had long been controlled by the bureaucracy, the military, royalist ideology, and a political system that had never permitted them a voice'. That was a new, more radical, form of politics that threatened the established structures of oligarchic rule. Thaksin's ultimate defeat in this tussle signalled the continuity of such rule.

Like the AEC, the pandemic created some opportunities for progressive elements to contribute to policymaking, especially in its early phases. This was in part due to the fact that, initially at least, the military government managed the pandemic well, making it possible for progressive elements to engage in street protests. But the government's use of repressive legal instruments combined with emergency powers has ultimately acted to stymie the scope for such protests, reducing progressive actors' influence (Auethavornpipat and Tanyag 2021).

7.2 Health Coverage

Prior to 2001, health insurance coverage in Thailand was low. The government provided generous health insurance benefits to civil servants, military personnel and their dependents through the Civil Servant Medical Benefit Scheme (from 1980), and less generous benefits to formal sector workers through the Social Security Scheme (SSS) (from 1990) (Ramesh 2000). But it offered limited coverage to other Thais. In 1975, it introduced a Low-Income Card (later renamed the Medical Welfare Scheme) to provide coverage to the poor, but this scheme was undermined by mistargeting and leakage. In 1983, the government introduced a Voluntary Health Card Scheme to provide coverage to informal sector workers, but this too failed to reach many of the intended beneficiaries. By the early 2000s, according to Nam (2015: 24), '30 percent of the population still lacked access to insurance coverage'. Many Thais, especially the poor and marginalised, were exposed to potentially catastrophic health costs.

The dominant oligarchy resisted the introduction of more generous health insurance arrangements for workers and the poor, using their positions to block initiatives, while progressive elements such as labour and NGOs lacked the resources and access to make headway (Ramesh 2000; Reinecke 1993). This balance of power proved to be a significant obstacle to the passage of the 1990 Social Security Act, the legislative foundation for the SSS and the third attempt to pass such legislation. It encountered strong resistance from elements in the military, the bureaucracy and, initially, the business community, and was finally passed only because the business elite shifted their position as part of a wider struggle to assert its dominance over the military-bureaucratic elite, who remained adamantly opposed (Reinecke 1993).

A more democratic constitution introduced in 1997, along with the devastating impact of the AEC, created new incentives for parts of Thailand's political elite to take up social protection policy, and new opportunities for progressive elements to mobilise for health insurance reform (Kuhonta 2017). The first election after the AEC, in 2001, saw Thaksin Shinawatra's *Thai Rak Thai* party elected on a platform including UHC, as well as resources for village development. The UHC policy and its speedy implementation were part of Thaksin's populist political appeal, bound up with an autocratic style of governing. But rather than being solely the result of Thaksin's agency, the UHC policy was nurtured and built by a coalition between progressive health bureaucrats and NGOs, many with links going back to the student democracy movement of the 1970s (Nam 2018).

Nam's detailed account reveals that progressive bureaucrats in the Ministry of Health had policy experience and a commitment to equity and poverty reduction; some had been involved in designing the health component of the SSS in 1990. They deliberately partnered with civil society groups in the health and wider development sectors, who had the capacity to mobilise grass-roots support for UHC. Together, this coalition mounted an advocacy campaign, explaining the idea, building enthusiasm and gathering signatures to present to parliament. The momentum they built convinced Thaksin of the popular appeal of universal health cover. His election as prime minister was thus their opportunity to push through long desired change. Once in government, they pressed for speedy implementation, both to head off opposition and to demonstrate the policy's success. The system was in place by mid-2002. The same alliance also developed the policy's key design features: a small 30-baht co-payment; using primary health care centres as gate-keepers; a capitation system allocating budgets to districts and hospitals on the basis of actual demand; and a separate National Health Security Office with an independent board including NGOs, to administer the scheme free of Ministry of Health interference. By 2015, the scheme provided around forty-eight million people with near-free access to health services, including hospitals. Alongside existing insurance coverage for civil servants and formal sector workers, that was close to universal coverage, including the informal sector and the poor, though excluding migrant workers (ADB 2019).

Thaksin's UHC scheme was attacked by mainstream economists and media outlets for being, as Kuhonta (2017: 94) put it, 'an electoral gimmick that would wreck the economy and lower the quality of health care'. But, since being introduced, it has proved remarkably durable. Despite the Thaksin government being overthrown in the 2006 coup and a successor government led by Thaksin's sister, Yingluck Shinawatra, being overthrown in a second coup in 2014, subsequent governments have defended, rather than moved against, the programme; the military government which replaced Thaksin not only maintained UHC but scrapped the 30-baht co-payment (Kuhonta 2017). Early in the pandemic, the current military government announced that the scheme would cover the cost of Covid patients, including in private hospitals.

As Hewison (2010: 130) commented about the wider impact of the Thaksin period (including his continuing polarising influence): 'arguably, his most thorough-going contribution was the embedding of ideas regarding state welfare. Subsequent governments have viewed welfare as essential for winning popular support from the grassroots'. Nevertheless, there was pushback from elements within the health ministry over a part of the scheme intended to redistribute resources. According to Kuhonta (2017: 110): 'a counterreaction by urban doctors and conservative bureaucrats in the Ministry of Public Health arose preventing the new financing structure from taking hold' by removing its incentives for doctors to move to rural areas. Despite this setback, the success of UHC in Thailand is a striking example of a well-prepared bureaucratic and CSO alliance being able to seize the opportunity when a window opened.

7.3 The Old Age Allowance

Thailand's old age allowance (OAA) was introduced in 1993. Initially, it took the form of a means-tested payment targeting a limited group of the poor, the 'underprivileged' aged sixty or over, without income, unable to work and without carers. At first there were only 20,000 recipients, with a very low level of benefit (Suwanrada and Wesumperuma 2012). The programme grew steadily over coming years and, by 2008, had 1.76 million beneficiaries. Yet, in the view of progressive elements such as HelpAge International, an NGO that seeks to promote the rights of elderly people, the targeted, means-tested nature of the scheme undermined its protective effects, and they called for it to be made universal (Wesumperuma 2009). At the same time, both progressive and technocratic elements were concerned about widespread misallocation in the programme, a problem that further supported the case for universality (Suwanrada 2009).

The distortion and misallocation under the scheme stemmed from the fact that local village representatives were delegated to identify who should be eligible, and there was no real central government effort to develop a targeting system. Reforms in 2005 gave local authorities even more discretion about decisions. There were consequently many reports of local conflict, favouritism and unfairness. One survey estimated that over 50 per cent of those who met the eligibility criteria were excluded from benefits, while unknown numbers were included through local cronyism (Suwanrada and Wesumperuma 2012). A World Bank report (2012: 18) described how local patron–client relations had distorted allocations: 'many recipients were not poor, but rather were related to selection committee members in the villages … As a result, the scheme had severe targeting problems and the concept of targeting was discredited'.

In 2003, Thaksin's government legislated to make the payment universal for all aged sixty and over who did not have a pension from another source, but it did not implement this change because, according to Paweenawat and Vechbanyongratana (2015), Thaksin simply had other priorities. It was only in 2009, under the Democrat party government of Abhisit Vejjajiva, that the OAA was made universal. The Democrats had returned to power after the tumultuous period following Thaksin's fall, after which Thaksin was banned from politics and found his party dissolved by the courts. Abhisit formed government in December 2008 promising a 'peoples' agenda', and in early 2009 declared that the social pension would be universal. Speaking at a forum organised by NGOs, including HelpAge International and other advocates of universal pensions, he argued that it was 'not populist policy, but rather a basic human right that everyone deserves. Social pensions promote income security in old age and the government is committed to ensure access to basic social pensions for all' (HelpAge International 2009). This support for income security from Thailand's oldest and most establishment-focused party reflects Hewison's point that governments after Thaksin have needed to appear committed to welfare. An immediate consequence of making the OAA universal was that the number of recipients increased substantially, to 5.65 million in 2010. In 2012, the *Pheu Thai* government of Yingluck Shinawatra then introduced different payment rates increasing with age. By 2019, the OAA benefitted over nine million Thais, at a cost of roughly 2 per cent of the total budget (Teerawichitchainan and Pothisiri 2021).

There is evidence the policy is popular. A survey conducted in 2011 asked if respondents preferred the pension to be universal or targeted, and whether they were willing to pay more tax to increase the benefits; 86 per cent favoured a universal payment, and 59 per cent both favoured universalism and were willing to pay more tax (Suwanrada et al. 2018). But there has been concern, especially from technocratic elements, about the costs, with the result that the government has kept payments modest. Those for people aged in their sixties are only 7.6 per cent of the national poverty line (Table 4). Because it is universal, any increase is very costly, and the rates had not increased for ten years until a temporary 'top-up' during the pandemic. The World Bank (2012: 18) has questioned the scheme's effectiveness in reducing poverty, noting that it 'provides benefits for all who are poor, but the majority of the benefits go to those who are not poor'. In 2016, these concerns led the Finance Ministry to announce it was considering withdrawing the OAA from individuals with an income greater than 9,000 baht per month, provoking criticism from advocates for the elderly (Knox-Vydmanov and Khiewrord 2016).

Contestation continued during the pandemic between progressive groups who supported universalism, political entrepreneurs seeking political advantage from a universal pension and technocratic elements concerned about the OAA's cost and effectiveness. In early 2021, there were reports that elderly recipients who had a pension from another source, but also illegitimately received the OAA, would be required to repay the latter. The Prime Minister, General Prayut, was quick to declare: 'I understand the plight of all the affected grandparents. You've done nothing wrong and neither have officials ... I will sort out the problems without you being taken to court or forced to return the money' (Thai PBS World 2021a). Even the leader of a junta – albeit one 'endorsed' by faulty elections in 2019 – has to be sympathetic to the elderly. And in September 2021, when there were reliable reports policymakers were again considering reverting back to targeting the OAA, welfare advocacy groups objected to this 'back-tracking' and the minister for Social Development and Human Security dismissed the idea as simply a 'rumour' (Charoensuthipan 2021). Thailand's universal pension – a very small payment that goes to very many – may well now be locked in.

8 Malaysia

8.1 The Political Settlement

Malaysia is by far the most developed capitalist economy of our case studies and has been the most stable politically. But the country's political settlement in recent decades has had many similarities to those of our other focus countries. The country has an oligarchic power structure characterised by the dominance of politico-business elites. During the first decade or so after independence, the ruling oligarchy comprised two distinct elements – a predominantly ethnic Malay political elite, most of whom were of aristocratic heritage, and a predominantly ethnic Chinese business elite. But, over time, the ruling oligarchy was 'reconstituted' as Malay nationalism grew stronger and the process of wealth accumulation proceeded (Khoo 2018; Khoo and Tsunekawa 2017: 12). The New Economic Policy (NEP) in 1970 was a key moment.

It sought to eradicate poverty and promote increased *Bumiputera* control over the economy. Under its framework, the government 'created state enterprises and acquired shares in well-managed, profitable companies to facilitate Malay ownership and provide managerial training' (Tan 2015: 201). The NEP protected such enterprises from competition and provided them with access to finance and subsidies. As Khoo (2018: 231) noted, these measures had a 'radically transformative' effect on the ruling oligarchy, leading to the emergence of new Malay oligarchs linked to the United Malays National Organisation (UMNO), the dominant party in the ruling *Barisan Nasional* (National Front) alliance.

Subsequent processes of privatisation during the 1980s and 1990s and financialisation from the 1990s onwards further enhanced oligarchic reconstitution by transferring state assets into the hands of well-connected Malay capitalists (in the case of privatisation) and enabling 'vast fortunes' to be 'made through the public listing of companies and Initial Public Offers, corporate mergers and acquisitions, and intense speculation in equities' (in the case of financialisation) (Khoo 2018: 231–2). In 1991, a 'Privatization Masterplan' was announced to shift away from Malaysia's traditionally prominent state role. Mahathir's slogan 'government has no business being in business' was applied to the total or partial sale of state railways, the national airline, telecommunications and energy generation. Corruption has been central to these processes, enabling political and bureaucratic figures and well-connected private and state capitalists to secure access to state licences, concessions and facilities or to simply pilfer funds from government or government-linked entities. These transactions were often without open tendering, leading, as Khoo (2012: 42) describes it, to a 'politically constructed market [where] rent-seeking behaviour and money politics were rife as coalitions formed around domestic conglomerates (sometimes with foreign partners) and powerful politicians who competed to become the chief beneficiaries of privatization'.

Technocratic figures have exercised significant influence over government policy, albeit much less than oligarchic elites. Khalid and Abidin argue these actors were largely 'side-stepped' at the micro-economic level – where oligarchic interests were more central – during Mahathir Mohamad's first premiership (1981–2003). Further, they became the 'instruments' of the political leadership, focusing on implementation rather than policy advice (Khalid and Abidin 2014: 387, 393). This reflected the fact that Mahathir had his own ideas about how state intervention and markets should combine to promote the country's economic development, the imperatives for state-driven redistribution associated with the NEP and privatisation, and the fact that Malaysia received relatively little foreign aid from the 1980s onwards, constraining the leverage of international organisations such as the World Bank and the IMF.

The technocrats' limited influence was highlighted by the government's heterodox response to the AEC: rather than following technocratic advice – including that of then deputy prime minister Anwar Ibrahim – to pursue IMF-style reforms, Mahathir adopted an alternative approach involving capital and exchange rate controls and expansionary fiscal policy (Liu 2001). However, technocratic figures were able to insulate certain areas of macroeconomic policy from oligarchic interference during Mahathir's first premiership (Booth 2001). And according to Khalid and Abidin (2014), technocratic figures exercised greater influence over policy under the subsequent governments of Abdullah Badawi (2003–9) and Najib Razak (2009–18), when the relevant figures were a new cohort of technocrats drawn from business schools and the corporate sector rather than their traditional base, the bureaucracy.

Finally, progressive civil society elements have exercised relatively little influence in Malaysia. As in other Southeast Asian countries, the period since the 1970s witnessed the emergence of a range of NGOs advocating for human rights, gender equality, consumer affairs, workers' issues, community development, democracy and good governance, some with a specific focus on health or education (Rasiah et al. 2017; Weiss 2003). But in general they have been excluded from meaningful participation in policymaking. The sacking of Deputy Prime Minister Anwar Ibrahim and his jailing on sodomy charges in the wake of the AEC triggered increased civil society mobilisation, the formation of new coalitions calling for change and increased engagement by civil society activists in party politics (Aspinall and Weiss 2012). But it did not precipitate the same shift in the balance of power between competing forces as occurred in Indonesia in the late 1990s, or the Philippines in the mid-1980s. The *Barisan Nasional* soon regained office after losing the 2018 election, albeit with a (possibly unstable) multi-party coalition. Continued *Barisan Nasional* rule has severely constrained opportunities for progressive elements to participate in policymaking.

The pandemic occurred in the midst of the fallout from the 2018 election result, making it difficult to distinguish its independent effects. But, as in our other focus countries, it appears to have tilted the balance of power slightly in favour of technocratic and progressive elements by shining a light on gaps in the country's social protection system, and encouraging technocratic and progressive elements to call for better social protection policies. As elsewhere, though, it has also precipitated moves by oligarchic elements to introduce new repressive measures or revive old ones to silence dissent (Sombatpoonsiri and Mahapatra 2021; Walden 2020). The overall effect has been to limit the extent of change in the political settlement.

8.2 Health Coverage

At independence, Malaysia had the foundation of an advanced health system. Rural primary health care was developed in the early 1950s under the British, as a deliberate policy of enticing Chinese villagers away from supporting the Communist insurgency during the Malayan Emergency. Others then demanded that 'the same attention to welfare be provided for indigenous peoples living in rural areas', leading to a nationwide Rural Health Scheme by the late 1950s (Wei et al. 2019: 39). Built on that base, Malaysian citizens have long been entitled to free primary health care in rural areas, with small co-payments for both urban health clinics and public hospitals. In this respect, Malaysia is a marked exception among our case studies, with universal health care for all (except migrant workers) in a public system. It meant that the state could factor in health, along with education, as existing social investments underpinning plans for industrialisation from the 1970s (Khoo 2012).

In turn, a high-quality and largely free health service has been crucial to maintaining the political support of the *Bumiputera* for the ruling elite. As Croke et al. (2019: 736) described this dynamic: 'UMNO first emerged politically to defend the position of the ethnic Malay community . . . throughout its history, UMNO has delivered a wide range of benefits to [them] . . . in exchange for their political support. Health is an important component of this relationship.' Ironically, that relationship and the popularity of a (largely free) health system have then been obstacles to the neoliberal agenda of privatisation that UMNO promoted especially during Mahathir's first premiership.

Attempts since the early 1980s to privatise parts of the health system, and to introduce a social insurance model of funding, have met significant civil society resistance. From 1983, Mahathir was keen on privatisation, arguing the standard public choice propositions about market competition, dynamism and affordability. As we have seen, in 1991 the 'Privatisation Masterplan' led to significant sale of state entities. In 1993, Mahathir declared the government could no longer afford free or heavily subsidised health care for all. Policy proposals to reform health financing have included compulsory insurance, private insurance and employer-funded schemes. But neoliberal reform attempts have largely failed. From 1994, 10 per cent of an individual's EPF balance could be withdrawn to pay for medical care and, from 2000, individuals could use their EPF savings to pay for private health insurance (Barraclough 2000). These were tentative methods to expand private health insurance, but the government's preferred option of a compulsory, contributory health insurance scheme has not been pursued.

There have been some steps towards privatisation of the public hospital system. Private doctors were given access to under-utilised public facilities, and haemodialysis clinics were contracted out to the private sector. In 1994, stores and laboratories in public hospitals were contracted out to a firm with links to UMNO, and in 1996, hospital support services (cleaning, laundry and maintenance) were contracted out to three providers, again with links to UMNO. There has been a significant expansion of the private system, including hospitals, medical clinics and dental clinics operating for profit, but public ownership remains high (Salleh 2012).

Barraclough (2000: 350) points to a key political restraint, namely the care UMNO 'must take ... not to alienate its principal constituency, the rural Malays, by appearing to diminish the welfare role of the government'. From 1998 consumer groups and the union movement formed a Citizens' Health Initiative coalition, opposing neoliberal reforms and argued for continued access to affordable health care, with support from the opposition parties. In the run-up to the 1999 election, privatisation of health care was a significant electoral issue, leading to the government backing off, and announcing extra funding for public hospitals (Barraclough 2000; Croke et al. 2019). Again in 2013, a proposal for a mixed private and public health insurance system was shelved as an election approached. Politicians that Croke and colleagues inter-viewed were aware Malaysians who 'already enjoyed near-universal access to publicly provided healthcare at modest cost . . . viewed reform attempts primar-ily as a threat'. United Malays National Organisation leaders acknowledged that given their reliance on the *Bumiputera* as a constituency, any change that diminished their benefits would be 'political suicide' (Croke et al. 2019: 733, 737). Smullen and Hong (2015: 352) point to a similar conclusion: 'the legacy of a strong government role in health care provision has created widespread societal support for maintaining the status quo'.

Coalitions of civil society organisations and opposition parties were import-ant in contributing to these debates, though the failure of the privatisation of health may have been less about a large-scale movement than about UMNO's extreme sensitivity to its *Bumiputera* constituency. In this case, the effect of democratisation – or the presence of democratic politics within a relatively authoritarian system – meant neoliberal reforms were resisted. Croke et al. note this is the reverse of what has happened elsewhere, where elites have blocked proposals for more equitable health care despite its popularity; democratisation had then broken that stalemate, triggering 'major health system reforms'. By contrast, the starting point in Malaysia was 'roughly the opposite' because the existing system was 'unusually progressive' (Croke et al. 2019: 737). The challenge for a neoliberal reform agenda was to convince citizens to surrender some of that progressivity. Croke et al. describe this as path dependence, as an instance of the status quo being locked in, resisting reform; but it may simply be citizens defending public goods they have against attempts to diminish them, and having sufficient democratic space to do so.

8.3 Income Support

Malaysia is classified by the World Bank as an upper-middle-income country, close to meeting its aspiration of becoming a high-income country. Yet with high-income status come higher expectations in social policy. The World Bank (2020a: 58) recently pronounced that 'to survive the [pandemic] storm and thrive in the "new normal" Malaysia needs an enhanced social protection system'; in 2018, Malaysia spent only 1 per cent of GDP on non-contributory social assistance programmes 'less than most upper middle-income countries'. Very little of Malaysia's social protection spending has been directed to the poor, who were expected to be lifted by a rising tide of economic development. In this context, the development of a new cash transfer scheme in 2012 was a marked departure from the patterns of the past, and was closely tied to the politics of reducing fuel subsidies, along with UMNO election strategising. When first introduced, the scheme was called 1 Malaysia People's Aid (*Bantuan Rakyat 1 Malaysia* or *BR1M*); it was renamed *Bantuan Sara Hidup [BSH]* in 2019.

Malaysia had long spent enormous resources on subsidising the cost of fuel; in 2012, for instance, fuel subsidies amounted to almost 14 per cent of the total budget. Such large budget commitments stifled other spending, and technocratic advisers saw it as a prime area for reform. As in Indonesia, fuel subsidies were severely regressive, with most of the benefit going to those on higher incomes with higher consumption. In 2009, it was estimated the richest 40 per cent of Malaysian households gained 60 per cent of the benefit, while the poorest 10 per cent received only 3 per cent (World Bank 2020a: 67). But, as in Indonesia, the politics of reducing fuel subsidies were delicate, because a price increase could have a significant impact on the poor, who could be mobilised to oppose change. It made sense – as in Indonesia between 2000 and 2009 – for the government to reduce fuel subsidies, while compensating the poor with cash transfers and hoping rent-seekers would not object as much as they had in Indonesia. At the same time, the cash transfer scheme provided new opportunities for UMNO to distribute benefits to key constituencies in the lead-up to elections, to enhance its re-election prospects.

The government announced BR1M as part of its 2012 budget. Najib Razak, who had been appointed Prime Minister in 2009 after Mahathir's successor resigned, was approaching his first election, due in May 2013. Weiss (2013) has suggested that BR1M was designed to help UMNO maintain support in rural areas where the cost of living was low and poverty high; a modest cash payment could thus make a difference to people's welfare. In September 2013, after its election victory, the government began making the case that reducing fuel subsidies would help the budget deficit, and that a targeted system of transfers would cushion the impact on the vulnerable, including UMNO's core constituency of rural Malays. There were protests by trade unions and consumer groups over rising fuel prices, and the main opposition parties were strongly opposed, arguing that corruption and transparency were more important issues to address (Bridel and Lontoh 2014). But with fuel subsidies becoming unsustainable, a subsidy reduction nevertheless went ahead, with substantial increases to the existing cash transfer system. The government subsequently used BR1M a number of times both to compensate the poor for the effects of economic reform the poor and to curry favour with key constituencies prior to elections. In 2015, for instance, it used the scheme to compensate for the introduction of a Goods and Services Tax. In early 2018, it pushed RM6.3 billion through the scheme in the lead-up to the crucial 2018 election.

At first, the cash transfers were targeted to households with incomes below RM3,000 a month, later raised to RM4,000, loosely defined as the lowest 40 per cent of households. Benefits vary depending on income, and are greatest for the poorest, at RM1,050 for a household earning less the RM1,000 per month. There is also a small allowance per child. By 2018, 7.1 million households were receiving the benefit, with the total expenditure representing about 2.2 per cent of budget spending. As Table 5 shows, for the poorest households, payments can be about 45 per cent of the National Poverty Line. *Bantuan Sara Hidup* is potentially a much more substantial redistribution of resources than the equivalents in Indonesia, the Philippines and Thailand (Choong and Firouz 2020; World Bank 2020a: 73).

The World Bank has provided a rare evaluation of *BSH*, which otherwise attracts little research attention. It found 92.8 per cent of B20 households (the poorest quintile of households) received the benefit; and 85.5 per cent of the bottom two quintiles received it, which left some, though not many, excluded. The report paid less attention to 'inclusion error', that is, to the ineligible who still managed to gain access, but it found that just over 40 per cent of the total funds were being distributed to the top three quintiles of the population (World Bank 2020a: 74). Despite this misallocation, the *BSH* programme is important as an instrument for poverty reduction, allocating significant funds to the poorest households. It has also been used for one-off cash transfers during the Covid crisis.

Alongside the smaller social pension, *BSH* represents the main element of Malaysia's social assistance effort. But while the cash transfer programme may effect some redistribution, the social pension is too narrow in eligibility ('breadth') to make a significant contribution. Given the evidence that the Employee's Provident Fund is unable to keep most retired workers from destitution, and given the failure of attempts to reform generous civil service pensions to put them on a more sustainable and less costly footing, the next stage of social protection development appears stalled. Welfare policy in Malaysia has stagnated rather than followed the typical path of rising with GDP per capita. With so little commitment to social welfare, stemming from the political dominance of oligarchic and, to a lesser extent, technocratic elements, Malaysia may struggle to negotiate a transition to a high-income society, with the sort of 'well-performing social protection system' that the World Bank regards as being 'a tool not only of social policy, but also an important part of wider economic policy' (2020a: 59).

9 Conclusion

Our primary argument in this Element has been that what does, and does not, get done in social protection in Southeast Asia has been largely governed by each country's balance of political forces. We have argued that our focus countries have, in general, been laggards in social protection development, particularly in those areas related to poverty and equity. There is a relationship between that underdevelopment, and the oligarchic and authoritarian nature of their regimes, especially before the AEC. Their particular political settlements – the balance of power between predatory/oligarchic, technocratic and progressive forces – have shifted over time, and in some cases in a direction that has favoured the latter two groups. Democratic reforms and economic and social crisis in the form of the AEC have been crucial in precipitating these shifts away from exclusionary political settlements towards more inclusive ones. Consequently, there have been some significant advances in social protection in the region and these have occurred against a general backdrop of substantial reductions in abject poverty. At the same time, the extent of advance has been held back by resistance from predatory elements as well as concerns by technocratic elements about the fiscal impact of reforms. Moreover, to the extent reform has occurred, it has meant layering progressive measures onto systems with pronounced conservative, productivist and predatory traits rather than more far-reaching or radical change.

In the early post-colonial period – when indifference to the condition of the mass of the people was commonplace – governing elites prioritised care for the civil servants and military on whom they relied for political support. The resulting pensions and health benefits were frequently very generous, with defined benefit pensions funded largely or entirely by the state. Reform in this area has been very difficult in the face of opposition from powerful beneficiaries. Attempts to slowly increase the retirement age have been tentative, especially in Indonesia, though more successful in Malaysia. Significant change to wind back the largesse established in the early pension schemes has only occurred in Thailand, and only for new entrants to the civil service since 1996, who have to make contributions and receive a less generous pension offer. When paying for the pensions and benefits of civil and military retirees is one of the first calls on the budget, these early decisions constitute a major and growing legacy from the past. To the extent that social protection needs to be about redistribution, this has been redistribution in the wrong direction.

Each of our case study countries also implemented a social insurance model of social security for formal sector workers, requiring regular contributions from employer and employee to cover old age, workplace injury and sometimes health care. But the model has only really worked in Malaysia; elsewhere it has been undermined by non-compliance and by very low rates of contributions. Especially in Indonesia, employers and workers resisted having to pay contributions. Even in Malaysia, where evasion was less severe, the savings in this social insurance experiment do not produce enough for adequate retirement. The effectiveness of this model of social protection has also been undermined by the fact that it is only of relevance to the formal sector workforce. In countries such as Indonesia and Thailand, with very large informal sectors, the social insurance model is anomalous. Both these earlier layers of social insurance – civil service/military pensions and formal sector savings schemes – are counted in the ADB and ILO data on 'social protection', but they are of no advantage to the least vulnerable in society.

Our focus countries also gave a high priority to FBE and health coverage. In the case of FBE, this was to expand access and, in so doing, reduce poverty and inequality, though FBE also served to ensure enough skilled and semi-skilled workers were available to support rapid industrialisation and economic growth in accordance with a productivist strategy. In Indonesia and the Philippines, the AEC and democratisation led to new efforts to extend and implement FBE as the crisis threatened school participation rates, progressive elements mobilised to demand change and political entrepreneurs promoted FBE in election campaigns. At the same time, however, progress towards FBE has been undermined by policies promoting the commercialisation and privatisation of education, continued underfunding of public education and continued corruption within the sector. These problems reflected the enduring political dominance in both countries of predatory elements as well as technocratic concerns to maintain fiscal discipline and promote the role of the private sector in education provision.

The political dynamics were similar in relation to health coverage. In Indonesia, the Philippines and Thailand, expansion of health coverage has been dramatic, especially in the latter case. Early initiatives in these countries were limited in scope and/or effectiveness. Important changes – such as UHC – developed in the context of new democratic openings, where actors with ideas and policies pressed for change and political entrepreneurs exploited the popularity of health coverage to enhance their electoral prospects. Our analyses of the Indonesian and Thai cases show there was resistance from oligarchic forces, but these ultimately lost control and could not put the genie back in the bottle. In Indonesia, notional extension of health coverage to the entire population with JKN from 2014 only occurred after vigorous resistance from business groups who objected to having to pay, and equally vigorous activism from part of the union movement and other civil society actors. The Thai case provides an illustration of a new political entrepreneur (Thaksin in 2001) working in a loose alliance with a network of health activists and bureaucrats, who were ready with policy proposals for an almost free, universal health system without the need for insurance premiums, and hence largely paid from the central budget. We saw that Hewison described the alliance behind Thaksin on this issue as including progressive bureaucrats and civil society and democracy activists, aligned against conservative bureaucrats, the Democrat party and the old business-military oligarchy. The former were able to seize the opportunity to implement a popular health care policy, and the latter could not reverse the initiative. In Malaysia, the politics of health coverage had different dynamics reflecting the early establishment of a national public health system. In that case, elite efforts to promote privatisation have run up against electoral imperatives stemming from the popularity of free public health care.

Income support schemes targeted to the poor – such as unemployment benefits, disability support, cash transfers and social pensions – have been less developed within the region, and often distorted in implementation. Targeted cash transfer programmes have been significant in Indonesia, the Philippines and Malaysia, and worked both as social stabilisers in times of economic disruption – especially fuel subsidy reductions in both Indonesia and Malaysia – and as pro-poor election promises with popular appeal. Cash transfer policies also have strong support from international agencies, concerned about social stability and poverty. Yudhoyono in Indonesia, with both unconditional and conditional cash transfers, and Aquino and Duterte in the Philippines with *Pantawid* were able to trade on the glow of significant transfer programmes that make some difference to redistribution towards poor families.

But these pro-poor programmes are only as good as their implementation and their distribution, and this is partly an issue of politics and also of expertise. The examples of social pensions in both Thailand and the Philippines show that lack of technical capacity, data and commitment to these challenges leaves an opening for local politics and patron–client relationships to distort allocation. Thailand faced the problem of misallocation in its Old Age Allowance, and solved it by making the allowance universal, although this meant very large numbers of people receive a very small payment, and made it prohibitively expensive to raise the level of payment for those who really need it. Some civil society activists have then fiercely supported a universal payment, and resisted technocratic attempts to trim the costs and target the pension.

The grossly distorted allocation of the targeted Social Pension in the Philippines meant significant funds flowed to those who did not need them, and who presumably knew they are not the intended beneficiaries. This reflected the power of predatory elements in the shape of small-scale patrons operating well below the level of the oligarchy. Compared with the epic and long-standing corruption of predatory elites, this is predation on a much smaller, even petty, scale, but it has much in common with the practice of the elites, and perhaps has learnt from their example. For those who work for progressive reform it is dispiriting to see a programme undermined by such predation.

As we have argued, the pandemic has caused major economic and social disruption, shone a light on major existing gaps, fuelled calls for change and forced governments to seek financial support from donors. It has led to additional social protection spending but mostly using existing mechanisms and most likely on a temporary basis. It does not so far appear to have triggered the reconfiguration in the balance of power that is required for a radical shift in the nature of social protection systems. Malaysia's government has been unstable, but this appears to be more about the break-up of the old UMNO ascendency. The Thai junta has faced significant pro-democracy street protests, and has responded with prosecutions for lese-majesty when protesters dare to think sovereignty comes from the people. Both Jokowi in Indonesia and Duterte in the Philippines have attempted to close down criticism, but the politics do not seem to be volatile.

Nevertheless, the politics of how the pandemic has been managed, or mismanaged, may have longer-term effects. We may find that under the emergency conditions of a pandemic, previously 'normalised' instances of corruption and neglect do more damage than usual to the stability of ruling elites in Southeast Asia. It may be that the sudden exposure to extreme vulnerability leads to renewed demands from citizens for more adequate social protection against future crises, and to movements for better, more equitable political settlements under which to live. But this remains to be seen.

Appendix

Timeline of Major Social Protection Developments

	Social insurance		Health coverage	Social assistance		FBE
	Civil service /military	Formal sector		Social pensions	Cash transfers	
1898						PHL: free compulsory education
1902	THA: civil service pensions					
1932						THA: four years compulsory education
1936	PHL: GSIS for govt. employees					
1939	MAL: civil service					
	THA: officials pension system – military scheme separated					
1943						PHL: free elementary education
1949		MAL: employees' provident fund				
1957		PHL: social security system	MAL: NHS for all			MAL: free primary education (Malays)
1960						THA: six years compulsory education
1962						MAL: free primary education (non-Malays)
1963	IND: Taspen (civil service pensions)					

1968		IND: Askes for civil servants	
1971	IND: Asabri – military scheme separated		
1972	MAL: military scheme separated		
1975		THA: low-income card (later renamed the medical welfare scheme)	
1977			IND: free primary education
1978			THA: free compulsory education
1980		THA: civil servant medical benefit scheme	
1982	MAL: Bantuan Orang Tua	THA: voluntary health card scheme	
1988			PHL: free secondary education
1990	THA: Social Security Act	THA: Social Security Act	

1992	
1993	IND: Jamsostek
1994	THA: old age allowance; IND: free junior secondary education
1995	PHL: PhilHealth for waged workers
1996	THA: government pension fund reform
1997	PHL: PhilHealth for 'sponsored' poor; THA: twelve years free and quality education
1998	THA: old age pension included in SSS
2000	IND: first unconditional cash transfers
2001	THA: universal health coverage
2003	IND: health insurance for some poor
2005	IND: expansion of UCT; IND: social assistance for older persons
2006	IND: school operational grants

(cont.)

Year					
2007				IND: PKH conditional cash transfers	
2008		IND: central Jamkesmas health insurance for some poor		PHL: first Pantawid conditional cash transfers	THA: fifteen years free and quality education
2009			THA: OAA universal		
2011			PHL: social pension		
2012				MAL: BR1M/ Bantuan Sara Hidup	
2013		PHL: PhilHealth for most of the poor			
2014		IND: BPJS Kesehatan			
2015	IND: BPJS Ketenagakerjaan			THA: child support grant	
2017				THA: welfare card	
2017				IND: program Sembako welfare card	

References

Abrahamson, Peter (2011) 'The Welfare Modelling Business Revisited: The Case of East Asian Welfare Regimes', in Gyu-Jin Hwang (ed.), *New Welfare States in East Asia: Global Challenges and Restructuring.* Cheltenham: Edward Elgar, 15–34.

Albert, Rose Ramon, Michael Ralph Abrigo, Francis Mark Quimba and Jana Flor Vizmanos (2020) *Poverty, the Middle Class and Income Distribution amid COVID-19*, Manila: Philippine Institute for Development Studies.

Anderson, Benedict (1988) 'Cacique Democracy in the Philippines: Origins and Dreams', *New Left Review*, 169: 3–31.

Anderson, Benedict (1990) 'Murder and Progress in Modern Siam', *New Left Review*, 181: 33–48.

Ansell, Ben (2010) *From the Ballot to the Blackboard: The Redistributive Political Economy of Education*, Cambridge: Cambridge University Press.

Arts, Wil A. and John Gelissen (2010) 'Models of the Welfare State', in Frank Castles, Stephan Leibfried, Jane Lewis, Herbert Obinger and Christopher Pierson (eds.), *The Oxford Handbook of the Welfare State*, Oxford: Oxford University Press, 569–83.

Association of South East Asian Nations (ASEAN) (2013) *ASEAN State of Education Report 2013*, Jakarta: ASEAN.

Asher, Mukul (2009) 'Provident and Pension Funds and Economic Development in Selected Asian Countries', in Katja Hujo and Shea McClanahan (eds.), *Financing Social Policy: Mobilizing Resources for Social Development*, London: Palgrave Macmillan, 264–89.

Asher, Mukul and Azad Singh Bali (2012) 'Malaysia', in Donghyun Park (ed.), *Pension Systems in East and Southeast Asia: Promoting Fairness and Sustainability*, Manila: ADB, 53–65.

Asia-South Pacific Education Watch (2007) *Philippines: Summary Report: Mapping Out Disadvantaged Groups in Education*, Mumbai: ASPBAE.

Asian Development Bank (ADB) (2012) *Asian Development Outlook 2012: Combatting Rising Inequality in Asia*, Manila: ADB.

   (2016) *The Social Protection Indicator: Assessing Results for Asia*, Manila: ADB.

   (2019) *The Social Protection Indicator for Asia: Assessing Progress*, Manila: ADB.

   (2021) *One Year of Living with Covid-19: An Assessment of How ADB Members Fought the Pandemic in* 2020, Manila: ADB.

Aspinall, Edward (2014) 'Health Care and Democratization in Indonesia', *Democratization*, 21(5): 803–23.

Aspinall, Edward and Meredith Weiss (2012) 'Limits of Civil Society: Social Movements and Political Parties in Southeast Asia', in Richard Robison (ed.), *The Routledge Handbook of Southeast Asian Politics*, London: Routledge, 213–28.

Auethavornpipat, Ruji and Maria Tanyag (2021) *Protests and Pandemics: Civil Society Mobilisation in Thailand and the Philippines During Covid-19*, Canberra: New Mandala, Australian National University.

Bah, Adama, Samuel Bazzi, Sudarno Sumarto and Julia Tobias (2019) 'Finding the Poor vs. Measuring their Poverty: Exploring the Drivers of Targeting Effectiveness in Indonesia', *The World Bank Economic Review*, 33(3): 573–97.

Barraclough, Simon (2000) 'The Politics of Privatisation of the Malaysian Health Care System', *Contemporary Southeast Asia*, 22(2): 340–59.

Barrientos, Armando (2013) 'Social Protection for Poverty Reduction: Approaches, Effectiveness and Challenges', in Katja Bender, Markus Kaltenborn and Christian Pfleiderer (eds.), *Social Protection in Developing Countries: Reforming Systems*, London: Routledge, 24–32.

Booth, Anne (2001) 'Initial Conditions and Miraculous Growth: Why is Southeast Asia Different from Taiwan and South Korea?' in Kwame Sundaram Jomo (ed.), *Southeast Asia's Industrialisation: Industrial Policy, Capabilities and Sustainability*, Basingstoke: Palgrave, 30–58.

Bridel, Anna and Lucky Lontoh (2014) *Lessons Learned: Malaysia's 2013 Fuel Subsidy Reduction*, Winnipeg: International Institute for Sustainable Development.

Business World (2010) 'Q&A: Views of Leadership', 30 April .

Cahyadi, Nur, Rema Hanna, Benjamin A. Olken et al. (2020) 'Cumulative Impacts of Conditional Cash Transfer Program: Experimental Evidence from Indonesia', *American Economic Journal: Economic Policy*, 12(4): 88–110.

Capuno, Joseph J., Aleli D. Kraft and Owen O'Donnell (2021) 'Filling Potholes on the Road to Universal Health Coverage in the Philippines', *Health Systems and Reform*, 7(2): e1911473.

Charoensuthipan, Penchan (2021) 'Old-Age Allowance Only for Poor Just a "Rumour"', *Bangkok Post*, 22 September.

Cho, Yoonyoung, Jorge Avalos, Yasuhiro Kawasoe, Doug Johnson and Ruth Rodriguez (2020) *Mitigating the Impact of COVID-19 on the Welfare of Low Income Households in the Philippines: The Role of Social Protection*, https://reliefweb.int/sites/reliefweb.int/, accessed 26 January 2022.

Choong, Christopher and Adam Firouz (2020) *Social Protection and Fiscal Policy in Malaysia*, Khazanah Research Institute Discussion Paper 9/20, Khazanah Research Institute.

Chuen, Roongkiat Ratanaban (2019) 'The Pension System in Thailand', *Nomura Journal of Asian Capital Markets*, 3(2): 34–9.

Civil Society Network for Education Reforms, Teachers and Employees Association for Change, Education Reforms and Solidarity, Maminturan Development Foundation, PUSAKA, USM-ACES Kabataan Kontra Kahirapan Philippine Human Rights Information Center; Asia South Pacific Association for Basic and Adult Education; and Global Initiative for Economic, Social and Cultural Rights (2016) *Privatization, Commercialization and Low Government Financing in Education: Infringing on the Right to Education of Filipinos, an Alternative Report submitted to the Committee on Economic, Social and Cultural Rights*, www .aspbae.org/wp-content/uploads/2022/10/HR-Parallel-Report-Privatization-Commercialization-and-Low-Government-Financing-in-Education-Philippines.pdf, accessed 7 April 2023.

Cook, Sarah and Jonathan Pincus (2014) 'Poverty, Inequality and Social Protection in Southeast Asia: An Introduction', *Journal of Southeast Asian Economies*, 31(1): 1–17.

Cortes, Josefina (1980) 'The Philippines', in Neville T. Postlethwaite and Murray R. Thomas (eds.), *Schooling in the ASEAN Region: Primary and Secondary Education in Indonesia, Malaysia, the Philippines, Singapore, and Thailand*, Oxford: Pergamon Press, 145–80.

Croissant, Aurel (2004) 'Changing Welfare Regimes in East and Southeast Asia: Crisis, Change and Challenge', *Social Policy and Administration*, 38(5): 504–24.

Croke, Kevin, Mariana Binti Mohd Yusoff, Zalilah Abdullah et al. (2019) 'The Political Economy of Health Financing Reform in Malaysia', *Health Policy and Planning*, 34: 732–9.

Dadap-Cantal, Emma Lynn, Andrew M. Fischer and Charmaine G. Ramos (2021) 'Targeting Versus Social Protection in Cash Transfers in the Philippines: Reassessing a Celebrated Case of Social Protection', *Critical Social Policy*, 41(3): 364–83.

Di John, Jonathan and James Putzel (2009) *Political Settlements*, Birmingham: GSDRC, University of Birmingham.

Editors (2021) 'Juliari's Ridiculous Sentence', *Jakarta Post*, 25 August, www .thejakartapost.com/academia/2021/08/24/juliaris-ridiculous-verdict.html.

Esping-Andersen, Gosta (1990) *The Three Worlds of Welfare Capitalism*, Cambridge: Polity Press.

Fineman, Mark (1987) 'Literacy Declining: Philippines: New Crisis in Education', *LA Times*, 21 November.

Gagne-Acoulon, Sandrine (2020) 'Philippines offers $600 for Information on Corrupt Officials', www.occrp.org/en/daily/12292, accessed 26 January 2022.

Ganjanakhundee, Supalak (2021) 'Thailand in 2020', *Southeast Asian Affairs*, 335–355.

Gonzales, Eduardo and Rosario Manasan (2002) 'Social Protection in the Philippines', in Adam Erfried, Michael von Huff and Marei John (eds.), *Social Protection in Southeast and East Asia*, Singapore: Friedrich Ebert Stiftung, 180–229.

Gough, Ian (2001) 'Globalization and Regional Welfare Regimes: The East Asian Case', *Global Social Policy*, 1(23): 163–89.

Haggard, Stephan (2008) 'Democratization, Crisis and the Changing Social Contract in East Asia', in Andrew MacIntyre, T. J. Pempel and John Ravenhill (eds.), *Crisis as Catalyst: Asia's Dynamic Political Economy*, Ithaca: Cornell University Press, 93–116.

Haggard, Stephan and Robert Kaufman (2008) *Development, Democracy, and Welfare States: Latin America, East Asia, and Eastern Europe*, Princeton: Princeton University Press.

Handra, Hefrizal and Astrid Dita (2016) 'Pension System and its Fiscal Implications in Indonesia', in Mukul Asher and Fauziah Zen (eds.), *Age Related Pension Expenditure and Fiscal Space: Modelling Techniques and Case Studies from East Asia*. Abingdon: Routledge, 104–36.

Hardjono, Joan, Nuning Akhmadi and Sudarno Sumarto (eds.) (2010) *Poverty and Social Protection in Indonesia*, Singapore: ISEAS.

Harson, Siktus (2020) 'Covid-19 and the Ugly Truth about Indonesian Education', 30 August, www.ucanews.com/news/, accessed 30 December 2021.

HelpAge International (2009) 'Thai PM Guarantees Older People's Right to Social Pension', 15 April, http://globalag.igc.org/pension/world/social/Thai.htm, accessed 24 December 2021.

Hewison, Kevin (2010) 'Thaksin Shinawatra and the Reshaping of Thai Politics', *Contemporary Politics*, 16(2): 119–33.

Hewison, Kevin and Garry Rodan (1994) 'The Decline of the Left in Southeast Asia', *Socialist Register*, 30: 235–62.

Hickey, Sam, Kunal Sen and Badru Bukenya (2015) 'Exploring the Politics of Inclusive Development: Towards a New Conceptual Approach', in Sam Hickey, Kunal Sen and Badru Bukenya (eds.), *The Politics of*

Inclusive Development: Interrogating the Evidence, Oxford: Oxford University Press, 3–35.

Holliday, Ian (2000) 'Productivist Welfare Capitalism: Social Policy in East Asia', *Political Studies*, 48(4): 706–23.

Holzman, Robert and Richard Hinz (2005) *Old-Age Income Support in the 21st Century: An International Perspective on Pension Systems and Reform*, Washington, DC: World Bank.

Hwang, Gyu-Jin (2012) 'Explaining Welfare State Adaptation in East Asia: The Cases of Japan, Korea, and Taiwan', *Asian Journal of Social Science*, 40: 174–202.

International Labour Organization (ILO) (2017) *World Social Protection Report 2017–2019: Universal Social Protection to Achieve the Sustainable Development Goals*, Geneva: ILO.

(2020) 'COVID-19: Impact on Migrant Workers and Country Response in Malaysia', May, www.ilo.org/asia/publications/issue-briefs/WCMS_741512/lang--en/index.htm.

(2021) *World Social Protection Report 2020–2022: Social Protection at the Crossroads – in Pursuit of a Better Future*, Geneva: ILO.

ILO-UN Women Collaboration (2015) *Facts and Figures: Women Migrant Workers in ASEAN*, Bangkok: ILO.

Jones, Catherine (1993) 'The Pacific Challenge: Confucian Welfare States', in Catherine Jones (ed.), *New Perspectives on the Welfare State in Europe*, London: Routledge, 198–217.

Karshenas, Massoud, Valentine Moghadam and Randa Alami (2014) 'Social Policy after the Arab Spring: States and Social Rights in the MENA Region', *World Development*, 64: 726–39.

Khalid, Khadijah Md and Abidin, Mahani Zainal (2014) 'Technocracy in Economic Policy-Making in Malaysia', *Southeast Asian Studies*, 3(2): 383–413.

Khan, Mustaq (2010) 'Political Settlements and the Governance of Growth-Enhancing Institutions', SOAS eprints, https://eprints.soas.ac.uk/9968/1/, accessed 6 February 2022.

Khoo, Boo Teik (2012) 'Development Strategies and Poverty Reduction', in Khoo Boo Teik (ed.), *Policy Regimes and the Political Economy of Poverty Reduction in Malaysia*, London: Palgrave Macmillan, 29–62.

(2018) 'Political Turbulence and Stalemate in Contemporary Malaysia: Oligarchic Reconstitutions and Insecurities', *TRaNS: Trans –Regional and –National Studies of Southeast Asia*, 6(2): 227–51.

Khoo, Boo Teik and Keiichi Tsunekawa (2017) 'Southeast Asia: Beyond Crises and Traps', in Khoo Boo Teik, Keiichi Tsunekawa, and Motoko Kawano (eds.), *Southeast Asia Beyond Crises and Traps: Economic Growth and Upgrading*, Cham: Palgrave Macmillan, 1–32.

Kim, Eunju and Jayoung Yoo (2015) 'Conditional Cash Transfer in The Philippines: How to Overcome Institutional Constraints for Implementing Social Protection', *Asia and the Pacific Policy Studies*, 2 (1): 75–89.

Kim, Mason (2015) *Comparative Welfare Capitalism in East Asia: Productivist Models of Social Policy*, Basingstoke: Palgrave Macmillan.

Kim, Sunhyuk (2015) 'NGOs and Social Protection in East Asia: Korea, Thailand and Indonesia', *Asian Journal of Political Science*, 23(1): 23–43.

Knox-Vydmanov, Charles and Usa Khiewrord (2016) 'Rationing the Old Age Allowance A Backwards Step', *Bangkok Post*, 27 May, www.bangkok post.com/opinion/opinion/990397/rationing-the-old-age-allowance-a-backwards-step.

Korpi, Walter (2006) 'Power Resources and Employer-Centred Approaches in Explanation of Welfare State and Varieties of Capitalism: Protagonists, Consenters, and Antagonists', *World Politics*, 58(2): 167–206.

Kuhonta, Erik (2017) 'The Politics of Health Care Reform in Thailand', in Ilcheaong Yi (ed.), *Towards Universal Health Care in Emerging Economies: Opportunities and Challenges*, London: Palgrave Macmillan, 91–118.

Kwon, Huck-Ju and Woo-Rim Kim (2015) 'The Evolution of Cash Transfers in Indonesia: Policy Transfer and National Adaptation', *Asia and the Pacific Policy Studies*, 2(2): 425–40.

Lane, Max (1990) *The Urban Mass Movement in the Philippines, 1983–1987*, Canberra and Singapore: ANU and ISEAS.

Lavers, Tom and Sam Hickey (2016) 'Conceptualising the Politics of Social Protection Expansion in Low Income Countries: The Intersection of Transnational Ideas and Domestic Politics', *International Journal of Social Welfare*, 25: 388–98.

Lee, Molly (1997) 'Education and the State: Malaysia after the NEP', *Asia Pacific Journal of Education*, 17(1): 27–40.

Liu, Olin (2001) 'Overview', in Kanitta Meesook, Il Houng Lee, Olin Liu et al., *Malaysia: From Crisis to Recovery*, Washington, DC: IMF, 1–2.

London, Jonathan (2018) *Welfare and Inequality in Marketizing East Asia*, London: Palgrave Macmillan.

Low, Choo Chin (2021) 'Legal Reforms in Protecting Migrant Workers' Welfare in Malaysia: Labor Law and Social Security', *Austrian Journal of South-East Asian Studies*, 14(1): 59–80.

Mietzner, Marcus (2020) 'Populist Anti-scientism, Religious Polarisation, and Institutionalised Corruption: How Indonesia's Democratic Decline

Shaped its COVID-19 Response', *Journal of Current Southeast Asian Affairs*, 39(2): 227–49.

Miller, Walter (1986) 'Aquino to Launch Campaign for New Constitution', *Atlanta Journal and Constitution*, 28 December: 30.

Moroz, Harry (2020) 'The Role of Social Protection in Building, Protecting, and Deploying Human Capital in the East Asia and Pacific Region', Social Protection and Jobs Discussion Paper No. 2008, Washington, DC: World Bank.

Murphy, John (2019) 'The Historical Development of Indonesian Social Security', *Asian Journal of Social Science*, 47(2): 255–79.

Nam, Illan (2015) *Democratizing Health Care: Welfare State Building in Korea and Thailand*, Basingstoke: Palgrave Macmillan.

(2018) 'Partnering for Universal Health Coverage in Thailand', *Asian Survey*, 58(2): 213–39.

Nino-Zarazua, Miguel, Armando Barrientos, Samuel Hickey, and David Hulme (2012) 'Social Protection in Sub-Saharan Africa: Getting the Politics Right', *World Development*, 40(1): 163–76.

Nixon, Stewart (2020) 'Commentary: What Struggling Malaysians Need from this Budget is a Stronger Safety Net – Higher Taxes', channel.newsasia.com/commentary: 5 November, accessed 10 December 2021.

Park, Donghyun (ed.) (2012) *Pension Systems in East and Southeast Asia: Promoting Fairness and Sustainability*, Manila: ADB.

Pascual, Federico D. Jnr (2021) 'Government Crooks Feast on COVID-19 Crisis', philstar.com/opinion, 26 September, accessed 10 December 2021.

Paweenawat, Sasiwimon Warunsiri and Jessica Vechbanyongratana (2015) 'The Impact of a Universal Old Age Allowance for Older Persons on Labour Force Participation: The Case of Thailand', *Population Review*, 54(1): 53–68.

Peng, Ito and Joseph Wong (2010) 'East Asia', in Frank Castles, Stephan Leibfried, Jane Lewis, Herbert Obinger and Christopher Pierson (eds.), *The Oxford Handbook of the Welfare State*, Oxford: Oxford University Press, 656–70.

Perez-Rubio, Bella (2020) 'Teachers' Group to DepEd: Revise 'Failed' Blended Learning Plan or Postpone Class Resumption', www.philstar.com/headlines/, accessed 24 January 2022.

Pernia, Ernesto and James Knowles (1998) 'Assessing the Social Impact of the Financial Crisis in Asia', EDRC Briefing Notes 6, Manila: ADB.

Phongpaichit, Pasuk and Chris Baker (2014) 'A Short Account of the Rise and Fall of the Thai Technocracy', *Southeast Asian Studies*, 3(2): 283–98.

Phongpaichit, Pasuk and Chris Baker (eds.) (2016) *Unequal Thailand: Aspects of Income, Wealth, and Power*, Singapore: NUS Press.

Pierson, Christopher (2005) '"Late Industrializers" and the Development of Welfare Regimes', *Acta Politica*, 40: 395–418.

Pineda, Edwin Shea (2019) 'The Philippine Pension System: New Buttresses for the Old Multi-Pillar Architecture', *Nomura Journal of Asian Capital Markets*, 3(2): 21–7.

Pisani Elizabeth, Maarten Kok and Kharisma Nugroho (2017) 'Indonesia's Road to Universal Health Coverage', *Health Policy and Planning*, 32: 267–76.

Pongsudhirak, Thitinan (2015) 'What's Next for Thailand?' www.weforum .org/agenda/2015/05/, accessed 10 December 2021.

    (2020) 'Top Brass, Technocrats, Politicos All Same', *Bangkok Post*, 12 June, www.bangkokpost.com/opinion/opinion/1933284/, accessed 23 January 2022.

    (2021) 'As COVID-19 Spreads, Thai Govt Stuck in Self-Made Trap', Irrawaddy.com/opinion/guest-column, 5 July, accessed 10 December 2021.

Prabhakaran Shreeshant, Arin Dutta, Thomas Fagan and Megan Ginivan (2019) *Financial Sustainability of Indonesia's Jaminan Kesehatan Nasional: Performance, Prospects, and Policy Options*. Washington, DC: Palladium, Health Policy Plus, and Jakarta: Tim Nasional Percepatan Penanggulangan Kemiskinan (TNP2 K).

Quimpo, Nathan (2005) 'Oligarchic Patrimonialism, Bossism, Electoral Clientism and Contested Democracy', *Comparative Politics*, 37(2): 229–50.

Quimpo, Nathan (2020) 'The Post-War Rise and Decline of the Left', in Toby Carroll, Shahar Hameiri and Lee Jones (eds.), *The Political Economy of Southeast Asia: Politics and Uneven Development Under Hyperglobalisation*, Cham: Palgrave, 133–54.

Ramesh, Mishra (2000) 'The State and Social Security in Indonesia and Thailand', *Journal of Contemporary Asia*, 30(4): 534–46.

Ramesh, Mishra and Mukul Asher (2000) *Welfare Capitalism in Southeast Asia: Social Security, Health and Education Policies*, Basingstoke: Palgrave Macmillan.

Ramos, Charmaine (2020) 'Change Without Transformation: Social Policy Reforms in the Philippines Under Duterte', *Development and Change*, 51(2): 485–505.

Rasiah, Rajah, Makmor Tumin, Latifa Hameed and Ibrahim Ndoma (2017) 'Civil Society Organizations in Opposition to Healthcare Commercialization: Protecting Access for the Poor and Middle Class in Malaysia', *Nonprofit and Voluntary Sector Quarterly*, 46(3): 567–85.

Reid, Ben (2008) 'Development NGOs, Semiclientelism, and the State in the Philippines: From "Crossover" to Double Crossed', *Kasarinlan: Philippine Journal of Third World Studies*, 23(1): 4–42.

Reinecke, Gerhard (1993) 'Social Security in Thailand: Political Decisions and Distributional Impact', *Crossroads: An Interdisciplinary Journal of Southeast Asian Studies*, 8(1): 78–115.

Rhoden, T. F. (2015) 'Oligarchy in Thailand?' *Journal of Current Southeast Asian Affairs*, 34(1): 3–25.

Riep, Curtis (2015) *Corporatised Education in the Philippines: Pearson, Ayala Corporation and the Emergence of Affordable Private Education Centers (APEC)*, Brussels: Educational International.

Robison, Richard (1986) *Indonesia: The Rise of Capital*, Sydney: Allen and Unwin.

Robison, Richard and Vedi Hadiz (2004) *Reorganising Power in Indonesia: The Politics of Oligarchy in an Age of Markets*, New York: RoutledgeCurzon.

Rokx, Claudia, George Schieber, Pandu Harimurti, Ajay Tandon and Aparnaa Somanathan (2009) *Health Financing in Indonesia: A Reform Road Map*, Washington, DC: World Bank.

Rosser, Andrew (2002) *The Politics of Economic Liberalisation in Indonesia: State, Market and Power*, Richmond: Curzon.

(2012) 'Realising Free Health Care for the Poor in Indonesia: The Politics of Illegal Fees', *Journal of Contemporary Asia*, 42(2): 255–75.

(2016) 'Neoliberalism and the Politics of Higher Education Policy in Indonesia', *Comparative Education*, 52(2): 109–35.

(2017) *Litigating the Right to Health in Indonesia: Courts, Politics and Justice*, Honolulu: East West Center.

Rosser, Andrew, Kurnya Roesad and Donni Edwin (2005) 'Indonesia: The Politics of Inclusion', *Journal of Contemporary Asia*, 35 (1): 53–77.

Rosser, Andrew and Ian Wilson (2012) 'Democratic Decentralisation and Pro-poor Policy Reform in Indonesia: The Politics of Health Insurance for the Poor in Jembrana and Tabanan', *Asian Journal of Social Science*, 40 (5–6): 608–34.

Rosser, Andrew and Anuradha Joshi (2013) 'From User Fees to Fee-Free: The Politics of Realising Universal Free Basic Education in Indonesia', *Journal of Development Studies*, 49(2): 175–89.

Rosser, Andrew and Priyambudi Sulistiyanto (2013) 'The Politics of Universal Free Basic Education in Indonesia: Insights from Yogyakarta', *Pacific Affairs*, 86(3): 539–60.

Rosser, Andrew and Mohamad Fahmi (2016) *The Political Economy of Teacher Management in Decentralised Indonesia*, World Bank Policy Research Working Paper no. 7913.

Rosser, Andrew and Maryke van Diermen (2018) 'Beyond Predatory Productivism? The Political Economy of Welfare Capitalism in Post-New Order Indonesia', in Hyun-Chin Lim, Jan Nederveen Pieterse and Suk-Man Hwang (eds.), *Capitalism and Capitalisms in Asia: Origin, Commonality, and Diversity*, Seoul: Seoul National University Press, 301–25.

Rudner, Martin (1977) 'Education, Development and Social Change in Malaysia', *South East Asian Studies*, 15(1): 23–62.

Salleh, Halim (2012) 'Welfare Regimes, Social Services and Poverty Reduction', in Khoo Boo Teik (ed.), *Policy Regimes and the Political Economy of Poverty Reduction in Malaysia*, London: Palgrave Macmillan, 145–82.

San Juan, David (2016) 'Neoliberal Restructuring of Education in the Philippines: Dependency, Labour, Privatization, Critical Pedagogy, and the K to 12 System', *Asia-Pacific Social Science Review*, 16(1): 80–110.

Schweisfurth, Michele, Lynn Davies, Lorraine Pe Symaco, and Oscar Valiente with Chelsea Robles (2016) *Developmental Leadership in the Philippines: Educational Experiences, Institutions and Networks*, Birmingham: Developmental Leadership Program.

Setijadi, Charlotte (2021) 'The Pandemic as Political Opportunity: Jokowi's Indonesia in the Time of Covid-19', *Bulletin of Indonesian Economic Studies*, 57(3): 297–320.

Sicat, Charlotte Justine and Maria Alma P. Mariano (2021) *Public Expenditure Review of Social Protection Programs in the Philippines*, Quezon City: Philippine Institute of Development Studies.

Sirindhorn, HRH Maha Chakra (2018) 'History and Development of Thai Education', in Gerald Fry (ed.), *Education in Thailand: An Old Elephant in Search of a New Mahout*, Singapore: Springer, 3–32.

Sjafrina, Almas and Dewi Anggraeni (2021) *Tren Penindakan Korupsi Sektor Pendidikan: Pendidikan di Tengah Kepungan Korupsi*, Jakarta: Indonesia Corruption Watch.

Smullen, Amanda and Phua Kai Hong (2015) 'Comparing the Health Care Systems of High-Performing Asian Countries', *Asia and the Pacific Policy Studies*, 2(2): 347–55.

Sombatpoonsiri, Janjira and Sangeeta Mahapatra (2021) 'COVID-19 Intensifies Digital Repression in South and Southeast Asia', https://carnegieendowment.org/2021/10/19/, accessed 23 January 2022.

Sparrow, Robert, Sri Budiyati, Athia Yumna et al. (2017) 'Sub-national Health Care Financing Reforms in Indonesia', *Health Policy and Planning*, 32: 91–101.

Streeck, Wolfgang and Kathleen Thelen (2005) 'Introduction', in Streeck and Thelan (eds.), *Beyond Continuity: Institutional Change in Advanced Political Economies*, Oxford: Oxford University Press, 1–39.

Sumarto, Mulyadi (2020) 'Insecurity and Historical Legacies in Welfare Regime Change in Southeast Asia – Insights from Indonesia, Malaysia, and Thailand', *Social Policy and Society*, 19(4): 629–43.

Suwanrada, Worawet (2009) 'Poverty and Financial Security of the Elderly in Thailand', *Ageing International*, 33: 50–61.

Suwanrada, Worawet and Dhamapriya Wesumperuma (2012) 'Development of the Old-Age Allowance System in Thailand: Challenges and policy implications', in Sri Wening Handayani and Babken Babajanian (eds.), *Social Protection for Older Persons: Social Pensions in Asia*, Manila: ADB, 153–67.

Suwanrada, Worawet, Pataporn Sukontamarn and Busarin Bankkaew (2018) 'Who Supports Intergenerational Redistribution Policy? Evidence from Old-age Allowance System in Thailand', *The Journal of the Economics of Ageing*, 12: 24–34.

Tadem, Teresa Encarnacion (2014) 'Philippine Technocracy and the Politics of Economic Decision-Making: A Comparison of the Martial Law and Post-Martial Law Periods', *Southeast Asian Studies*, 3(2): 345–81.

(2018) 'Technocracy and Class Politics in Policy-making', in Mark Thompson and Eric Batalla (eds.), *Routledge Handbook of the Contemporary Philippines*, London: Routledge, 261–71.

(2020) 'The Emergence of Filipino Technocrats as Cold War "Pawns"', *Journal of Contemporary Asia*, 50(4): 530–50.

Tan, Jeff (2015) 'Rent-Seeking and Money Politics in Malaysia: Ethnicity, Cronyism and Class' in Meredith Weiss (ed.), *Routledge Handbook of Contemporary Malaysia*, London: Routledge, 200–13.

Teerawichitchainan, Bussarawan and Wiraporn Pothisiri (2021) 'Expansion of Thailand's Social Pension Policy and its Implications for Family Support for Older Persons', *International Journal of Social Welfare*, 30: 428–42.

Thai PBS World (2021a), 'How a Flaw in the System Lands Thailand's Elderly in Trouble', www.thaipbsworld.com/ accessed 30 December 2021

Thai PBS World (2021b) 'Will COVID-19 Give Birth to a Welfare State in Thailand', thaipbsworld.com/ 25 March, accessed 10 December 2021.

Thompson, Mark (2010) 'Reformism vs. Populism in the Philippines', *Journal of Democracy*, 21(4): 154–68.

Transparency International (2020) *Global Corruption Barometer Asia: Citizens' Views and Experiences of Corruption*, Berlin: Transparency International.

United Nations Development Programme (UNDP) (2016) *Leaving No One Behind: A Social Protection Primer for Practitioners*, New York: UNDP.

United Nations Economic and Social Commission for Asia and the Pacific (UNESCAP) (2018a) *Social Outlook for Asia and the Pacific: Poorly Protected*, Bangkok: UNESCAP.

(2018b) *Inequality in Asia and the Pacific in the Era of the 2030 Agenda for Sustainable Development*, Bangkok: UN.

UNESCAP and ILO (2021) *The Protection We Want: Social Outlook for Asia and the Pacific*, Bangkok: UN.

United States Agency for International Development (USAID), Education Quality and Access for Learning and Livelihood Skills (EQuALLS) and Education and Livelihood Skills Alliance (ELSA) (2007) *Policy Research on Access to Quality Basic Education for Muslim Learners*, Washington, DC: USAID.

Vaghefi, Negin, Fatimah Kari and Muzulwana Abdul Talih (2017) 'Poverty and Income Replacement Profile among EPF Retirees in Malaysia', *Social Indicators Research*, 132: 1065–78.

Valenzuela, M. Rebecca (2000) 'Asian Crisis and the Philippines: Counting the Social Costs', in T. Van Hoa (ed.), *The Social Impact of the Asia Crisis*, Basingstoke: Palgrave Macmillan, 17–33.

Van Diermen, Maryke (2017) *Welfare in Motion: The Politics of Social Protection in Indonesia*, PhD Thesis, Adelaide: University of Adelaide.

Velarde, Rashiel B. and Jose Ramon G. Albert (2018) *The Socpen and its Role in Closing the Coverage Gap among Poor Elderly Filipinos*, World Bank Social Protection Policy Note 14.

Villegas, Bernardo (2021) 'Addressing the Philippine Education Crisis', *Business World*, 23 June: S1/7.

Walden, Max (2020) 'Malaysia Stares Down Health, Political Crises as Anwar Ibrahim Strikes Back', www.abc.net.au/news/2020-10-06/, accessed 23 January 2022.

Wei, Justen Wong Han, Ng Chiu Wan and Su Tin Tin (2019) 'Malaysia's Rural Health Development: Foundation of Universal Health Coverage (UHC)', *Jurnal Sains Kesihatan Malaysia*, 17(1): 31–41.

Weiss, Meredith (2003) 'The Malaysian Human Rights Movement', in Meredith Weiss and Saliha Hassan (eds.), *Social Movements in Malaysia: From Moral Communities to NGOs*, London: Routledge: 140–64.

Weiss, Meredith (2013) 'Malaysia's 13th General Elections: Same Result, Different Outcome', *Asian Survey*, 53(6): 1135–58.

Wesumperuma, Dharmapriya (2009) 'Pension Fund: "Social Pensions" Ensure Income Security in Old Age' *Bangkok Post*, 20 January, www.pension-watch.net/knowledge-centre/?guid=4d4d28a367f29&order=n.

Widoyoko, Danang (2011) 'The Education Sector: The Fragmentation and Adaptability of Corruption', in Edward Aspinall and Gerry van Klinken (eds.), *The State and Illegality in Indonesia*, Leiden: KITLV, 165–88.

Williams, Geoffrey (2021) 'Time for a National Social Assistance Fund to help the Poor', freemalaysiatoday.com/category/opinion: 13 October 2021, accessed 10 December 2021.

Winters, Jeffrey (1996) *Power in Motion: Capital Mobility and the Indonesian State*, Ithaca: Cornell University Press.

Winters, Jeffery (2012) 'Oligarchs and Oligarchy in Southeast Asia', in Richard Robison (ed.), *The Routledge Handbook of Southeast Asian Politics*, London: Routledge, 53–67.

Wisnu, Dinna (2007) *Governing Social Security: Economic Crisis and Reform in Indonesia, the Philippines and Singapore*. PhD Thesis, Columbus: Ohio State University.

World Bank (1988a) *The Philippines Education Sector Study: Part One: Overview and Summary*, Washington, DC: World Bank.

(1988b) *The Philippines Education Sector Study: Part Two: Technical Chapters and Annexes*, Washington, DC: World Bank.

(1998) *Education in Indonesia: From Crisis to Recovery*, Washington, DC: World Bank.

(1999) *Country Assistance Strategy of the World Bank Group for the Republic of the Philippines*, Washington, DC: World Bank.

(2000) *Health Strategy in a Post-Crisis, Decentralizing Indonesia*, Washington, DC: World Bank.

(2001) *Social Protection Sector Strategy: From Safety Net to Springboard*, Washington, DC: World Bank.

(2012) *Reducing Elderly Poverty in Thailand: The Role of Thailand's Pension and Social Assistance Programs*, Bangkok: World Bank.

(2014) 'Extending Protection to the Poor Where the Needs are Greatest', www.worldbank.org/en/results/2014/04/28/, accessed 3 November 2021.

(2018a) *Philippines: Social Protection Review and Assessment*, Washington, DC: World Bank.

(2018b) *Case Study of the Employees Provident Fund in Malaysia*, Kuala Lumpur: World Bank.

(2020a) *Malaysia Economic Monitor, June 2020: Surviving the Storm*, Kuala Lumpur: World Bank.

(2020b) *Philippines Basic Education: Public Expenditure Review*, Washington, DC: World Bank.

(2021) *Regaining Lost Ground, Revitalizing the Filipino Workforce*, Taguig City: World Bank.

WHO (2022) 'Coronavirus Dashboard', https://covid19.who.int/ accessed 3 September 2022.

Yarrow, Noah and Rythia Afkar (2021) 'Rewrite the Future: How Indonesia can Overcome the Student Learning Losses from the Pandemic and Increase Learning Outcomes for All', https://blogs.worldbank.org/eastasiapacific/, accessed 24 January 2022.

Yuda, Taufid (2020) 'The Development of "Islamic Welfare Regime" in South East Asia: Drawing Experiences from Brunei Darussalam, Malaysia, and Indonesia', *International Journal of Sociology and Social Policy*, 40(3/4): 220–35.

Acknowledgements

We wish to thank the editors of the Cambridge University Press Elements series on Politics and Society in Southeast Asia, three anonymous reviewers and David Lozada for their feedback on an earlier version of this manuscript. We also wish to thank Bahruddin Bahruddin for his research assistance.

Cambridge Elements

Politics and Society in Southeast Asia

Edward Aspinall

Australian National University

Edward Aspinall is a professor of politics at the Coral Bell School of Asia-Pacific Affairs, Australian National University. A specialist of Southeast Asia, especially Indonesia, much of his research has focused on democratisation, ethnic politics and civil society in Indonesia and, most recently, clientelism across Southeast Asia.

Meredith L. Weiss

University at Albany, SUNY

Meredith L. Weiss is Professor of Political Science at the University at Albany, SUNY. Her research addresses political mobilization and contention, the politics of identity and development, and electoral politics in Southeast Asia, with particular focus on Malaysia and Singapore.

About the Series

The Elements series Politics and Society in Southeast Asia includes both country-specific and thematic studies on one of the world's most dynamic regions. Each title, written by a leading scholar of that country or theme, combines a succinct, comprehensive, up-to-date overview of debates in the scholarly literature with original analysis and a clear argument.

Cambridge Elements $\equiv$

Politics and Society in Southeast Asia

Printed in the United States
by Baker & Taylor Publisher Services